Wolf Blass, behind the bow tie is published by Fairfax Books, which is a division of Fairfax Media Limited. Any opinions expressed in this book are those of the author and Fairfax Media does not intend by this book to provide any endorsement or recommendation of any particular products, organisations or companies.

The Sydney Morning Herald is a registered trademark of Fairfax Media Publications Pty Ltd
The Age is a registered trademark of The Age Company Ltd

Publisher Fairfax Media Publications Pty Ltd
Cover picture Randy Larcombe
Internal pictures Randy Larcombe, Tim Williams, George Fetting, Eddie Jim, Peter Schofield, AFP/A Morozov, Fairfax Media archive and Wolf Blass' personal archive

For distribution, copyright and marketing enquiries, contact Caroline Lowry on (02) 9282 3582

For production enquiries, contact Peter Schofield on (03) 9601 2149

Printed in Australia by McPherson's Printing Group
ISBN 978-1-921486-13-5

WOLF BLASS

Behind the Bow Tie

The Man ~ The Brand ~ The Foundation

LIZ JOHNSTON

AUTHOR'S NOTE

In assisting with the research for this authorised biography, Wolf Blass provided a list of names of those people who have been important to him throughout his life. He was surprised by some statements, amused by others and disagreed with some. But he made no substantial changes to the original manuscript before approving it for publication, and those dealt mainly with facts and figures. This was another surprise to many who have known him as a control freak in every aspect of his life. "There are a lot of contradictions in Wolf, he's a complex personality," his wife, Shirley Nyberg-Blass, says. "There is also a little boy in him that needs controlling and discipline." Perhaps, in having a stranger look into his world by talking to others, Wolf hopes to get a better view from within of the brand he has created for himself and his wines. Or perhaps, as his wife says, he just needs to be noticed. Whatever the reason, he makes for a good story.

Liz Johnston

ACKNOWLEDGEMENTS

First of all, my thanks to Liz Johnston for her skill and clarity in writing the story of my life and weaving the information provided into an accurate and comprehensive account. This would not have been possible without the extensive, initial interviews conducted by Ross Muller. Thanks also to my personal assistant Judi Prosser for her dedicated coordination of this project since inception.

A special thanks to my beautiful wife Shirley for her support, patience and understanding during the consuming task of documenting my history, revealing aspects of my life not previously published.

My sincere gratitude to all those who were interviewed and contributed to this book, whose lives were interwoven with mine and enriched my journey.

From a professional perspective, I would also like to acknowledge the many wonderful people who have underpinned the success of the Wolf Blass brand and made it a global icon – grapegrowers, winemakers, cellar hands, production managers, technical and engineering staff, secretaries, label designers, marketing and sales staff, distributors, wine judges, media, and most of all the loyal consumers. I salute you!

A special thanks must go to Ian Hickinbotham who was responsible for bringing me to Australia by offering me a contract with Kaiser Stuhl.

And finally, thank you Australia for making it all possible.

I think the most enjoyable professional experience and challenge in my life has been to achieve those things that many critics said couldn't be done. I am not satisfied with second best!

Wolf Blass

CONTENTS

Many words and descriptions spring to mind when one is asked to talk of, or indeed introduce, Wolf Blass. Sadly, many such as "icon" which may well describe Wolf, are over used and abused these days. I think the words "larger than life" best sum him up. You are never left wondering or in doubt about where Wolf is focused or what's on his mind. The motto "Carpe Diem" was seemingly imprinted on his brain from a very early age.

In this book we read of his early years, revealed to many for the first time. His upbringing, the war years, the hardship experienced in schooling and his early professional life, all provide a solid foundation for Wolf's desire to not only seize each day, but every opportunity that is offered or opens.

His zest for life, plain speaking, straight to the point, determined, focused and sometimes outrageous nature, belie an underpinning sense of honesty and integrity. Wolf regards these latter two characteristics as paramount in his life to date.

It is these solid beliefs and energy that have seen him not only develop his own career and business interests, but the careers and businesses of many others, especially in the wine industry. Wolf's contribution to the Australian wine industry is legend.

His entrepreneurial skills, innate sense of branding and effervescent character have provided added dimension to this nation's wine industry. The improvements in variety, range, quality and exports as well as the introduction of wine to new markets can often see its genesis in what Wolf has done and achieved. Indeed, I was delighted to present his Membership in the Order of Australia to him when Governor of South Australia in 2001, as it was for his service to the development of the Australian wine industry, particularly as an exporter, the promotion of excellence in winemaking, viticulture, marketing and research. In my view it marked due recognition by the people of Australia for the contribution by a young German migrant who arrived here in 1961 and has never stopped contributing as a true Aussie! (Though he is still adept at complicating the English language!)

I think that once again we must look to Wolf's early years to understand why he is such an energetic worker for his community. His love of, and empathy

with, people from all walks of life sees him contributing and giving back to a diverse range of organisations, bringing his unique levels of humour and energy to everything he does. Lists of activities and associations may be found elsewhere, as they take up a number of pages. I have personally observed his unique talents to organise, enthuse, motivate, entertain, guide and succeed in many community projects and am pleased to be one of his RASCALS, an eclectic group of men who enjoy good food, good wine and good company.

Wolf is larger than life, unique, one out of the box, a gem and many other descriptors. To his mates he is simply a good bloke.

Never have you ever met, or ever likely to meet, anyone quite like Wolfgang Blass AM!

Sir Eric Neal AC CVO

This book is dedicated to my

wonderful family.

Success has little to do with speed, but much to do

with direction, passion and ambition.

WOLF BLASS

The Governor-General of the Commonwealth of Australia, being the representative in Australia of Her Majesty Queen Elizabeth the Second, requests all those whom it may concern to allow the bearer to pass freely without let or hindrance and to afford him or her every assistance and protection of which he or she may stand in need.

AUSTRALIA
PASSPORT
Type-Type AUS
State-Staat
PASSPORT Nr. 6453276

Surname/Nom
BLASS
Given names/Prénoms
WOLFGANG FRANZ OTTO
Nationality/Nationalité
AUSTRALIAN
Date of birth/Date de naissance
02 SEP 34
M
Place of birth/Lieu de naissance
SITZENRODA GERMAN
Date of expiry/Date d'expiration
08 MAY 86

Herr
Frau
Fräulein
erhält die Erlaubnis, nach Ablegung der Prüfung*)
ein Kraftfahrzeug mit Antrieb durch
Verbrennungsmaschine
der Klasse – eins – zwei – drei – vier*)
zu führen
Bad Kreuznach, den   195
Stadtverwaltung
Kfz.-Zulassungsstelle
Im Auftrage:
Liste Nr.
ap. Stadtinspektor
*) Nichtzutreffendes ist zu streichen.

Vermerk des amtlich anerkannten Sachverständigen oder
Prüfers für den Kraftfahrzeugverkehr.*) **)
Nach bestandener Prüfung ausgehändigt.
Bad Kreuznach, den 4 März 1958
Der amtlich anerkannte Sachverständige/Prüfer*)
für den Kraftfahrzeugverkehr
Liste Nr.
(Unterschrift)
*) Nichtzutreffendes ist zu streichen.
**) Bei Führerscheinen der Klasse 4, bei erneuter Erteilung nach Entziehung
der Fahrerlaubnis und in den Fällen des § 10 Abs. 3 StVZO ist dieser Ver-
merk gegebenenfalls zu streichen.

Eigenhändige Unterschrift des Inhabers:

Lieu
Height
Taille
Colour of Hair   Dark Brown
Couleur des Cheveux

CHILDREN
ENFANTS
Place and Date of Birth
Lieu et Date de Naissance
X X X
Name
Nom

PHOTOGRAPH OF BEARER
PHOTOGRAPHIE DU TITULAIRE

Issued at   Adelaide
Délivré à
on   31 Dec
le
and valid for five (5) years
et valable pour cinq (5) an
An Officer duly auth
Passport
Bearer should sign
SIGNAT
SIGNAT
Bearer's attention is drawn to
IMPORTANT information on
inside back page of passport.
3

The Governor-General
Australia, being the rep
of Her Majesty Queen
requests the bearer to pass freely with
and to afford him or her eve
protection of which he or she may stand in

PASSPORT
Type-Type AUS
Code
State
AUSTRALIA
DOCUMENT No.
E7513718
BLASS
WOLFGANG FRITZ OTTO
AUSTRALIAN
02 SEP 34
M
18 MAR 97   SITZENRODA
18 MAR 07
ADELAIDE

Chapter 1

ONLY A BLOODY BOY

They called him The Black One, winning favours with his impish nature. Wolfgang Franz Otto Blass (above in 1936 and opposite) was born into a wealthy, respected family in the village of Stadtilm in the Thuringia Mountains in East Germany.

It is the winter of 1945 and a thin, cherub-faced boy of 10 or 11 in a ragged German military uniform is watching as the end of his part in World War II straggles past, a line of human misery. He has stolen food and fuel from the Nazis and will later rob the foxholes left behind by the advancing Americans. Small and dark – they called him The Black One – at age six he had become a favourite of the local commander of the Military Supply Depot in his hometown village in East Germany, his impish nature winning him special favours.

Throughout World War II, Wolf Blass' maternal grandfather and mother, Irmgard, had kept open the long-established family villa and the attached Otto Sohn bottling factory complex. Grandfather Otto Sohn, the most influential person in the life of the boy and later the man, had maintained the business and negotiated his way through the red tape of war, providing generous amounts of schnapps and wine to civil and military officials.

In later years, the boy would do the same in faraway Australia, where it was always known that "Wolfie" had a car filled with good wine for sharing. Here, instead of the German card game skaat that his grandfather played weekly with the powerbrokers of the town, Wolf would play football with passion, drive vintage cars and enjoy horseracing – all the perks of a young society that ultimately repaid him with wealth and public acknowledgment for his achievements in its once unknown wine industry.

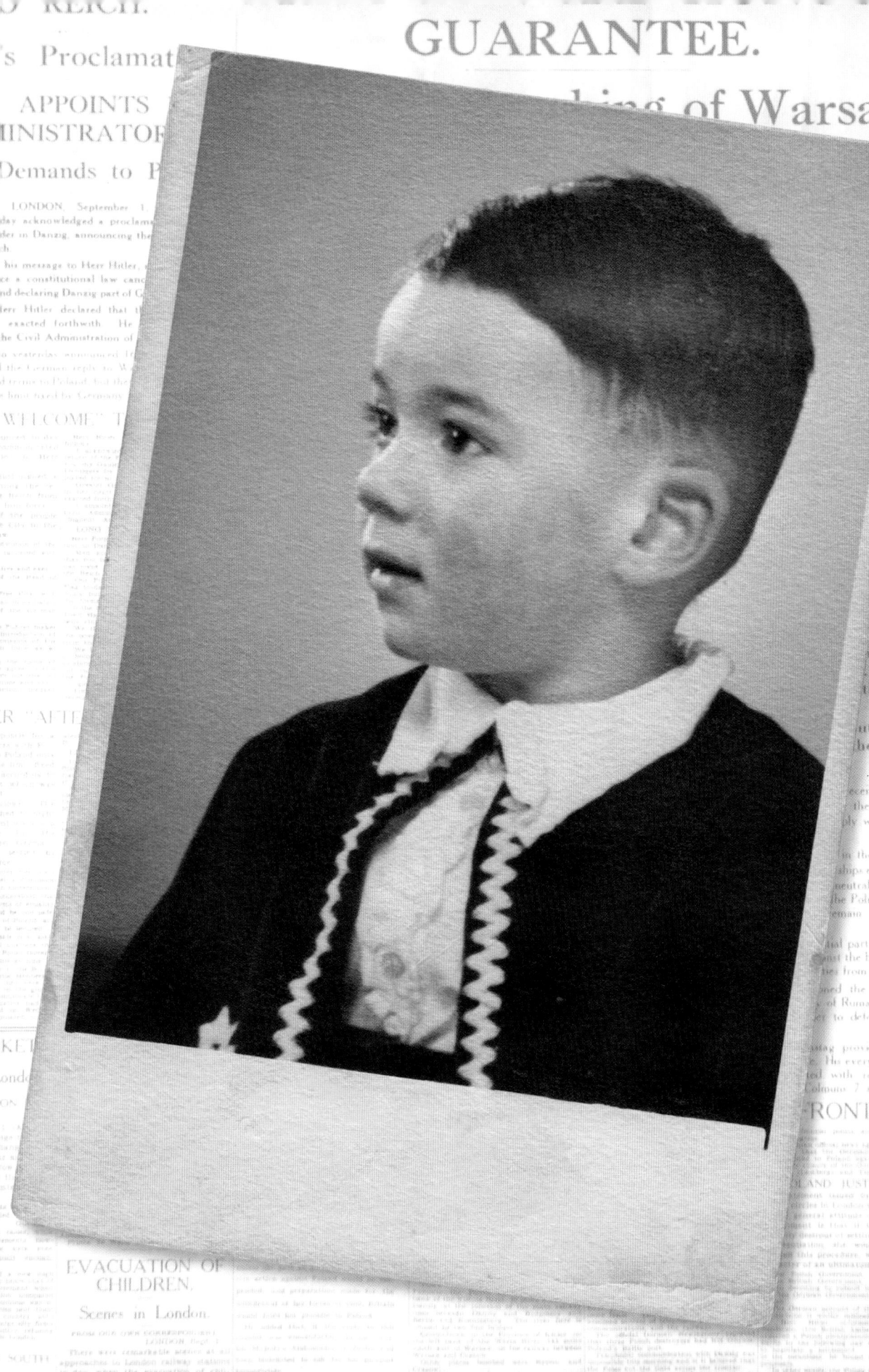

Wolf as a boy in
military uniform.

Wolfgang Franz Otto Blass was born in 1934 – "a Virgo in a good vintage year" – into a wealthy, respected family in the village of Stadtilm in the Thuringia Mountains. His mother's father had the wine and spirit business and his father, Friedrich, was a doctor of law and economics. His mother's family lived in a large, luxurious villa at the edge of the village, beside the bottling factory and above the deep, cool wine cellars. The young, super-active boy led an idyllic life in a valley that is one of the most naturally blessed in Germany, with its rivers and lakes, steep mountains and dense, green forests.

He was five when war broke out in 1939 and far too young to be aware of the havoc it could wreak on his world, even though he must have realised the men of the household were gone, his uncles to the front and his father to an administrative position in Berlin. The years 1942-43 were good for the family business: Germany was winning the war and, though the men of Stadtilm had gone, French prisoners of war supplied sufficient labour to keep the plant running. Of course, the tide turned and by the winter of 1945 grandfather Otto Sohn was negotiating with the German soldiers planning a last stand at his factory gates in the path of the advancing Allies.

"They had the order to defend, but for some reason or another it wasn't done, and I think – when history declares all this – that my grandfather actually was responsible for the

town of Stadtilm not being rolled over," recalls Wolf. "They had plans to blow up everything. They wanted to dig around our property, which was at the end of the town, to defend it if the tanks were rolling in. This would have seen a total demolition of the houses and factories and everything else. They were absolutely bloody stupid, because there were two mountains and Stadtilm was sitting in the middle. So they would have defended from one side and the Americans come in from the other. "

As the Allies drew nearer, young Wolf noticed more and more military officers and members of the local hierarchy visiting the family complex. "My grandfather had more parties and shows and all this type of thing. At the time I didn't really realise what was going on, what happened, but this was part of the softening of the local military attitude. My grandfather convinced them it would be useless to make a defence system. And here again I remember that the negotiations at the end of the war took place around my grandfather, that it must have been the schnapps, the brandy or cognac or whatever the thing was that convinced them to move the unit away."

Wolf did not come across death firsthand until the war's final days. He had seen and heard the bombs dropping, listened to and read the reports of the dead and dying. But with Friedrich working in Berlin and his uncles at the front,

Grandfather Otto Sohn, the most influential person in the life of the boy and later the man, provided generous amounts of schnapps and wine to civil and military officials during the war.

Wolf's grandfather, mother, aunts and cousins remained sheltered behind the walls of their complex. This early life – absent father, a mother consumed by the need to keep the business running and a grandfather forever networking and juggling competing interests to keep a large number of dependent women and children safe – was to have a profound, some would say even tragic, effect not only on his marriages but also on his own children years later in Australia.

Wolf's third wife, Shirley Nyberg-Blass, believes the inevitable tensions of this kind of childhood affected Wolf so much emotionally that he has never understood the concept of family, and in turn has never dealt well with emotional issues involving family members.

Perhaps he learned early that emotion was something to be traded on and taken advantage of. Next to the family bottling factory was the Military Supply Depot, where luxury items from occupied countries were stored – Wolf particularly remembers the chocolates from France, Italy and Belgium. He was such a favourite of the commander in charge of the stores that he even had a special military uniform made up for him to wear. "He took me as a mascot. He

Wolf was a favourite of the local Nazi commander, who even had a special military uniform made up for him to wear. "He took me as a mascot."

Friendly adults, a generous source of chocolate – any young boy, anywhere, would have been happy with this. But it was a grace-and-favour situation, not one of mutual respect and affection. The control was not in Wolf's hands and the power of his mentor was backed by the awesome authority of the military. This might be why, as an adult, Wolf has never willingly given up control of any part of his life, whether in business or marriage.

Nevertheless, when he moved to London in the 1950s, Wolf hid his identity, aware that the stain of Nazi Germany went with him. "Because of my age and nationality, English people had to be treated very carefully. People thought I was Rhodesian and I didn't deny it. But, you know, in Germany I was only a bloody boy, I mean, you have to look at this from a different bloody angle."

There was one chilling example in the final days of war of what had been going on outside the family compound. As the Allies drew closer, the Nazis began to clear prisoners from Buchenwald, just a few kilometres from Stadtilm and one of the largest German concentration camps with more than 130 satellite labour sites. It is thought some 65,000 of an estimated 250,000 prisoners perished here from 1937 to 1945, including 11,000 Jews.

The earliest inmates were political prisoners, prisoners of war from many nations, resistance fighters, criminals, former government officials

said I was a very nice bloke. And I had a German uniform they had made for me and, despite the fact that it was always guarded, the whole bloody place, you know, I could almost walk in and out. You have to look at it from the point of a child who likes to play Indians or play soldiers."

As a kid in a war zone you

become a street fighter. The survival

kit is built into you.

WOLF BLASS

of German occupied countries, Jehovah's Witnesses, Roma and Sinti gypsies and German military deserters. In 1945, there were 112,000 prisoners and the camp supplied forced labour in armaments factories and stone quarries and on construction projects. The SS staff sent those who were too weak or disabled to work to euthanasia facilities or they were killed by phenol injections administered by the camp doctor.

None of this was known to young Wolf, even on that day in 1945 when he watched with his cousins as the Germans began to evacuate 28,000 prisoners from the main camp and several thousand more from the labour satellites. About a third of them died from exhaustion en route or soon after arriving. Or they were shot by the SS.

"We were standing down at the gates and we saw this big, big column. It was the marching of the concentration camp people. And we kids were standing there and we asked the question,

What was it all about? We were told, 'They are criminals'. And they were shot, you know, anybody who was weak, bang, was shot. And they were left there and when the Americans came they were still there. And we thought, 'Oh, they are real criminals, they deserve no better'. But the corpses were left – left and right – on the road. The occupation forces made the Germans pick them up."

Looking back through the prism of a long and successful life outside of Germany, Wolf believes that, as a child, he didn't really know anything of the horrors perpetrated at Buchenwald. "You know, it only came to me later on because a very close friend, Hans Richter, is living in Singen in southern Germany where there is a death march plaque and suddenly it hit me again, when I saw that. I knew what happened then. I stood back and I said to my brother, Fritz, 'No, you were littler, this is what happened, this is when all these guys marched past our gate…' But they didn't march, they were crawling, and then as soon as their weakness started they were shot – bang – and they left them there. First of all we thought they were all criminals, because they had these striped outfits on and then we said, 'Oh, they wanted to escape'. Of course they couldn't escape, they were too bloody weak, they couldn't bloody run. The story from our elders, not my uncles, I mean, there was no men there, they would have bloody made the thing, like, that's how it is."

Wolf has returned to the plaque at Singen a few times since to learn more. "How many got killed? I have got it all on this big plaque, I have got the photo and I said, 'You know, it is just one of the things.' And the impression probably hit me much later."

Toward the end of the war, the adults listening covertly to the British Broadcasting Corporation knew that Germany would soon be defeated. But for the children, especially Wolf, who was five when war broke out, life had always been lived at the behest of the Third Reich. Thuringia was the first German state to embrace Hitler's National Socialist Party and the most important region to the armament industry during the war. In 1943, it was producing huge numbers of aircraft and spare parts. The world-famous Carl Zeiss optical company produced binoculars, distance-measuring devices and submarine optical sights.

Their most important products were optical devices for anti-aircraft weapons. The Thuringian glass industry was the main supplier of glass ampoules for the German army medical service.

None of which would have been of interest to a child, even one of Wolf's lively nature. For him life was an adventure and, although it was dangerous, he revelled in it and developed a set of skills that he says undoubtedly fitted him for success later on.

It was probably inevitable that if Wolf was to prosper it would be down to the things he learned as a child raised in a war. "As a kid in a war zone you become a street fighter. The survival kit is built into you. You become very smart from the word 'go' because, you know, food is very important and during the war you needed to know something about the black market, because money didn't exist. I think it had something to do with having seen the darkness; the bright side was in front of me and I had a vision that one day I would get somewhere, but I just never knew in which direction." By the time he was 11, he was qualified at least for a career in break-and-enter and petty theft. Had the war not ended, he would have been drafted into the Youth Brigade at 12.

Once a week, Otto Sohn would break out the cards in his office and play skaat with the pastor and the mayor. "The office was locked and of course the schnapps was there and the wine was there and they were all having a good

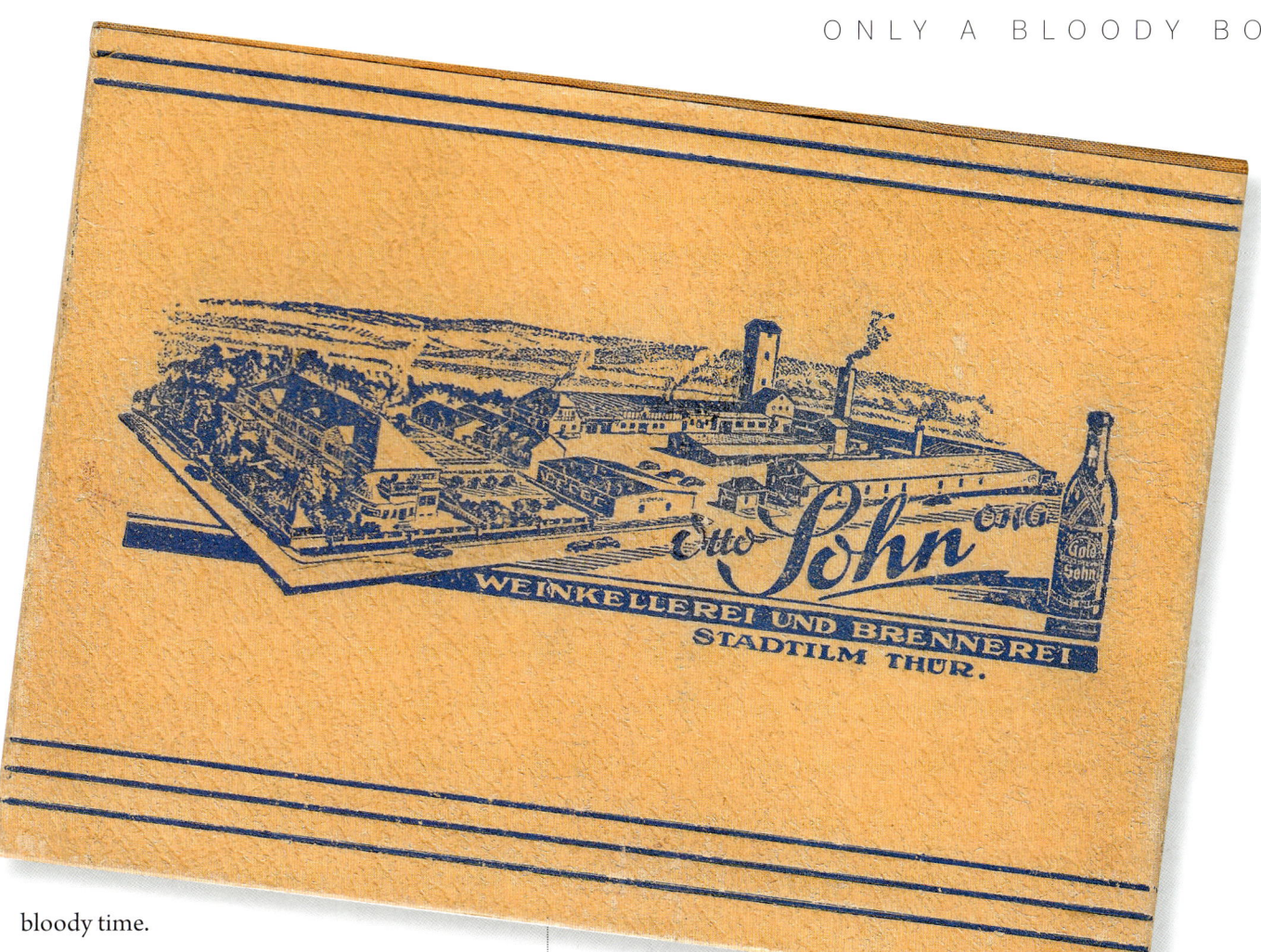

bloody time.

But I was allowed to come in and next to this place he had a safe room where he had stuff which was not available, secret cigars and all this type of thing, and it was locked and nobody could get in. But my brother and me, we went through the back section of the window and he must have known what was going on because things disappeared all the time."

Obviously, that thrill wasn't big enough because Wolf and his brother and their friends became more adventurous. Initially, it wasn't particularly out of a need for food, though. "You could have enough to eat. My grandfather was very smart. He'd had a very close association with these people and, of course, if we had wine and spirits things were going quite easy." His job was to carry wine and brandy around the villages, trading it for food from surrounding farms.

Still, there was an army warehouse that intrigued the boys in his little gang of four or five. "It was huge. It used to be a cable factory, but it was stopped during the war and was being used for food storage. And I had another friend, Manfred Walter, who was a couple of years older and he was always looking after me. He said, 'Nobody's touching me, punching me up.' So we

Throughout the war, Wolf Blass' grandfather and mother kept open the family villa and the attached Otto Sohn bottling factory complex at Stadilm.

raided this warehouse. We went in, filled up our bloody bags and just shot out again. This was all for some excitement. But it could have got you also into trouble. Because you're a kid you don't think. Later on, of course, you become smarter."

By 1944, the military administration was in chaos, and the Allies' Spitfires were flying in as low as 150 metres, targetting the storerooms next to the family villa. "If anything moved, it didn't matter what it was. If you had a horse or a cart or any blooming thing, it was knocked around." The Allies also targetted the rail viaduct at Stadtilm.

"This became a nightmare also for the train service, but that was where 'WB' was the smart cookie again. When they started the bombardments and fired into the supply train system, blew up the trains, all the carriages were full. With these trains, you never knew what was on them. Was it food, was it clothing, was it supply? These planes were going up and down, bloody firing from about one-and-a-half kilometres away, and right up to the train station at Stadtilm, and then they'd turn around and do it all again. And when they turned we just got onto the train to see what was there.

"This one day, I had a big bag and I thought it was peas, green peas, and each time these planes turned I grabbed my bloody stuff – you couldn't let go because somebody else would have bloody pinched it in the meantime – and we went back into cover; the planes came down again, and then they turned around. So I walked this one-and-a-half-kilometre length of track, running each time when the planes came and then throwing myself on the ground. This was in an open field near my home, you know, not in the city."

Wolf got home and presented Irmgard with the spoils of his day dodging the fighter planes. "Oh, she shit herself, first of all, you know, said I was running outside there when all this bloody

Having seen the darkness, the bright side was in front of me. I had a vision that one day I would get somewhere, but I just never knew in which direction.

WOLF BLASS

nonsense was going on, and I gave her this bag and I said here is some peas, but it wasn't, it was green coffee beans." For a coffee fanatic forced to rely on chicory substitutes for years, it must have been difficult for Irmgard Blass to keep scolding her boy about risk taking.

Certainly, it was the first time Wolf had revealed the boy who would become the man who loves to please women. "My mother was so happy to have coffee I went back to get some more. But then the military police were there and so it wasn't as easy."

Still, there were opportunities further afield. The sound of bombardment within riding distance would always have Wolf and his friends on their bicycles to check out what might be available. By this time, school no longer played much part in the lives of the children of Stadtilm, and Wolf and his friends continued free-looting across the Thuringia Valley. There were still rules that had to be obeyed, even as the Third Reich crumbled. "You had to, 'Sieg Heil, Heil Hitler' to whatever elders were left in the city, most of them were administrators or something like this."

There was also a shortage of fuel and food from 1944 onwards, adding necessity to the thrill-seeking career of the boys' thieving, which was only enlivened by the night bombing raids on Berlin and the city of Arnstadt, about 12 kilometres away. "We thought it was a little bit of fun when the night bombing began because

they were flying over our town and you had the search lights going and all that. We didn't really take this very seriously, we took it as a game. The seriousness came after this, when the day bombardments were taking place.

"We could actually see the oxygen zone stripes up in the sky and you just shook your blooming head, you said, 'Have a look what the … ' You could see actually where they were dropping the bombs because they were dropping tracers and they looked like Christmas trees with all the lights on them. Bang!"

As the Allied fighting forces advanced, there was another ready source of treasure for the young adventurers. "When the Americans were moving in we were bloody walking around all

Wolf's mother, aunts and cousins remained sheltered behind the walls of their family complex, where his grandfather entertained the local hierarchy. "Of course, if we had wine and spirits things were going quite easy."

If somebody asked me for one word to

describe Wolf, I would say 'fearful'.

SHIRLEY NYBERG-BLASS

through the forest, and bloody picked up the guns, and we were shooting around and doing the most incredible things. I mean, the Americans had everything. They were on the move, but they had all the supplies. We had nothing, so we actually went into the foxholes, wherever they were, and we just followed the bloom'n fighting and just picked everything up which was left there. All the emergency rations, chewing gum, cheese, bickies and all this type of thing. You did things which were so stupid that you can't believe this has all happened."

The war years undoubtedly provided the foundation for Wolf's legendary confidence in his ability to set his own course in the face of all opposition. But throughout those years there was always a home base at the villa – even without the men and the women working to keep 10 children from various families fed – and when the war ended Wolf was to endure some of the unhappiest times of his life.

"During the war we all lived together in a huge villa and there was an underground walkway, so you had a connection from the upstairs to the underground cellars. You know, that was always a lot of fun. Then I remember I was the oldest in the whole big family conglomerate. I was always the dictator, I dictated everything that was going on. So I wasn't very popular with my cousins and everybody else." Childhood pictures show young Wolf sitting regally in a small wagon, his cousins dragging him along. "And I was sitting in there and probably thought that I was going to be in a royal coach!"

Interestingly, although at the end of his life, Wolf the Australian Wine King assumes a sort of egalitarian royalty in his lifestyle, some friends and colleagues hint that there's also a trace of benevolent dictatorship in the Barossa Valley, where began the Wolf Blass brand and his vision to turn Australians, in particular the women, into wine lovers.

Either way, for many years after the war life for the young Wolf was less than royal. "My upbringing was unfortunate, coinciding with World War II. And the disaster and the chaos which took place in 1944-45 with the breakdown of the Deutsche German Reich. There was no food, there was no employment, there was no commerce, no industry left, and I had to experience the American, the French, the British and then the Russian occupation."

One of his worst experiences was at the hands of a German called Edmund Diehl. When he finished school, Wolf's father found him his first job, at 16, as an apprentice labourer on a mixed farm owned by the former high-ranking party member of the Reich. "It was the toughest time of my life. You wouldn't believe how this has hounded me, almost in my dreams, and I can't understand this. As a result I became very ambitious. I wanted to get on the top."

That journey to the top ended at the bottom of the world in Australia, but 60 years later Wolf was still dealing with the demons of his childhood. As an adult, he began returning to Germany regularly to attend a health farm. He also began to revisit scenes of his youth. As an adult, he read deeply about World War II and Germany's role in it. The scenes of the Death March he had watched as a child came back to him and the true story – not what he was told as a boy, that these people were criminals – suddenly became clear to

him when he stood years later with Fritz in front of that memorial in Singen. "That's what I saw."

Turning 75 in 2009, Wolf talked about letting go of a few responsibilities. At the same time, he was preparing a schedule that would see him travelling almost constantly around the world for most of the year to celebrate the launch of his 75th Birthday Tribute Wines by Foster's, the global wine giant that saw a golden opportunity to own Australia's leading brand in 1996 and bought the company.

More importantly, Foster's recognised the value of the man himself as a living legend and retained him as an official ambassador to the world for Wolf Blass Wines.

But behind the loud bow ties that he has made his trademark in Australia, behind the self-proclamations of his greatness that became synonymous with his name, there is a different, less confident man. "If somebody asked me for one word to describe Wolf, I would say 'fearful'," Shirley Nyberg-Blass says of her husband of 20 years. But fearful of what?

"Wolf would hate to be forgotten," Shirley says. "I think he feels he has to be noticed. He needs to be out there or people will forget about him. But, as much as he wants to be known, there are times that he really needs to get away from it because he doesn't want to talk. But then once you've got yourself out there it's a little bit hard to become a shrinking violet, isn't it?" WB

Chapter 2

GERMANS SURRENDER, BLASS CONQUERS BRITAIN

After years of war, how does one surrender to the conquering armies marching through town? The rules of disengagement are not usually familiar to people about to be taken over by a force that for five years has been trying to destroy them and everything they own? What was the right timing? Should they run into the streets and risk being shot by the remnants of their own defeated army? Should they hang out white flags, the age-old sign of surrender that seemed archaic – bizarre even – in the face of the sophisticated weaponry used in the war just ended. Wolf remembers many discussions in the family – his father had returned home by then and would soon find himself collecting the death march corpses littering the roadside as the Americans rolled in. "It had to be at the right time. It was a touch and go situation."

Once again, grandfather Otto Sohn knew how things would go. "He always assembled himself with the right people, to find out what was going on. Later on, it was quite clear to me, with the affiliation he had in wine, drinking and food and everything else, and the parties he threw in the big villa, that this gave him the security, because he wasn't even in a party – this is the amazing thing. Later on, he also had the same affiliation with the Americans and with the Russians."

On his grandfather's advice, it was decided to hang white bed sheets out the windows of the villa and all the houses. In the Otto Sohn cellar, where the extended family had been living for days as the Allies marched in, everyone knew

A Soviet soldier in front of the destroyed Reichstag building in Berlin, May 1945. When the Russians arrived, "It was a very different picture to the Americans with their cars and jeeps."

this must not be done too soon. "If you were going to surrender and there was still a German army there, you were shot," Wolf says. Finally, they heard American voices: "Hey there, yeah, yeah, yeah, come on, get out."

"And then we saw the first American soldiers. So we knew that was the end and the beginning of something else. I'm quite sure there was not a big fuss about the whole thing. They had to go looking and calling into the houses. Everybody had to come out and they kept marching on."

Then, with no police, no authority yet established, the looting began. And the first target was the Otto Sohn factory with its precious bounty of wine and spirits and cigarettes. "It was women, mostly, who pulled out their carts and went to the factory and filled up with bloody things ... lots of booze and everything else." The Americans were close behind in enjoying the pleasures of the villa. "They took our grandfather's section and made this the headquarters for the whole town. Us kids weren't involved at all. I think my grandfather must have moved to his other sons' homes or something."

The Americans loved the complex with its aged teak timber and vast internal spaces; they loved the huge garden, instantly setting up barbecues, to the astonishment of the children. This was also the first time the youngsters had seen bananas and tropical fruits and, except for the bigger boys like Wolf who'd already been on raiding parties to the American foxholes, they

were enthralled by chewing gum, a concept quite beyond those for whom food had been a scarce resource rather than for chewing and discarding. "And there were the emergency ration packs with cigarettes and biscuits and all these things just flying around blooming everywhere."

The natural reaction for the youngsters would have been obvious to anyone aware of their recent adventurous past. "Of course, we tried to see if we could steal whatever we could." It was not the best move in terms of good relations with the conquerors. These were the first troops to arrive, the fighting troops, not the occupying forces. The fighting was still going on in Germany and the surrender of Stadtilm was a local one only, not an official surrender. It would be another two weeks before the fall of Berlin.

For a week the Americans laughed as they threw cigarettes into the street and watched people falling over each other to grab them. In turn, the local people watched in wonder as the Americans cooked up great mounds of meat – schnitzel and steaks – or poured litres of precious fuel into a hole and set fire to it. "Everything was upside down, there was no system of what belonged to you or didn't belong to you, it was just bad. A bad experience of not knowing where, what, how, because you couldn't really move. But it was a peaceful situation, there was no fighting in Stadtilm then, although you could hear the grenades and some tanks rolling and everything else, but this was a long way away. The bombing wasn't important anymore, there was nothing more to bomb, I suppose. We were all finished. There were no more movements. Even in the end, you didn't see much German transport system shifting. I don't think there was much left."

The Americans became more assertive once they had been in Stadtilm for about a week, in a bid to restore some order to the free-for-all looting. "Butchers, bakeries, anything was looted." At the same time the attitude of the Americans created tension. "They had definitely a superior attitude as victors, there was no doubt about this. It was an unpleasant situation. It didn't affect us kids as much, but the generosity wasn't there as it had been to begin with."

When the American fighting forces moved out of Stadtilm, the French occupation forces moved in for a few weeks and, after them, the English. "Sure, it was confusing, but that's how it is when you are on the losing side." Then the Russians arrived. "There were hundreds and hundreds of infantry and they were all sitting on cars and on the horse trucks, lying there with straw and everything. It was a very different picture to the Americans with their cars and jeeps."

Again, Wolf and his friends were bystanders as history marched along the highway, this time a different sort of death march, that of democracy as East Germany was handed to the Russians, who had arrived in a long, winding

> *We knew that this was the end and the beginning of something else.*
>
> WOLF BLASS

column from the east. "Their police were on horse flesh on each side, galloping backwards and forwards to make this a very smooth entry. And we were saying, 'The Russians are coming, something terrible is going to happen.'" The initial Russian occupation was peaceful, but then the investigations of the locals' political activities during the war began. And so did the drinking. "Drinking was one of their main priorities. And I think they weren't really as disciplined as they could have been, so you had to be a little bit careful as a grown-up to manoeuvre around wherever they were, and they were everywhere."

Once again, the Otto Sohn villa was taken over as headquarters. "That was bad, having the schnapps and vodka and everything else which was produced there. It was a little bit of a nightmare. In the meantime, of course, the ex-German warehouse supply system was suddenly also opened. So there was a real circus about

US forces cross the Roer River into Germany in 1945. "Everything was upside down, there was no system of what belonged to you or didn't belong to you."

who was getting what and the Russians clamped down."

Wolf remembers the winter night the Russian soldiers came and took the warehouse manager and his father and some other men away in their pyjamas. "They put them on the tractor and they drove them off about three kilometres and I thought that that was the end, that they would get shot for some reason. Then they knocked them all around, and the father lost all his teeth. I don't think they intended to kill them, just to scare them, have some fun." The threatening visits recurred and eventually Wolf's mother came close to breaking point and it was decided to move from

the main house into the warehouse buildings, the former cable factory that a younger Wolf had so mischievously broken into under the Germans.

It was also decided by grandfather Otto that Wolfie, who had been running wild for much of his young life, should settle down to some serious school work. "My grandfather was actually the man who probably had most to do with my life. He was a highly successful, determined operator and he always protected me, despite the fact that I was on the loose 90 per cent of the time. His discipline, his professional activity, which I can still remember, would have had a bearing on me, because I never had any affiliation, really, with my father. My father was never there, but my grandfather was always on the stand-by. I had become, for a while, lost in the family system and I had to get out of the way of that.

"So my grandfather organised that I went to the former Adolf Hitler Sports School, which is in Wickersdorf in the central Thuringian. I went to boarding school from the end of '45 till up to '46. That was one of the most disciplined bloody schools, then controlled by the Russians. So my grandfather probably thought that would be a good thing for me to go there."

But Wolf and a friend decided to run away. They had very little money and each carried a small suitcase as they set off to walk through the forest to the nearest railway station. "We walked through the forest so we would not be detected, because they'd start looking for us. They would know that we were not there, because you had to report in the morning and in the evening – a typical regimental school system."

The two boys rode in a coal wagon, leaving it just before the border of the Russian sector in order to escape detection. "We had no permit, we had nothing, and on the end station in the Russian sector there was a big control with a pass system, so anybody was arrested who was there without authority. So we again started tramping through the forest at night and then we had to go through some villages and I remember when the Volks Polizei – the People's Police – were

marching through this village. It was the last village before we had to go across a very steep forest mountain. We had to go into a pig sty, or some bloody sty, and we had to get in there and we could actually hear these guys when they were marching and how they moved."

Yet, as Wolf remembers it, neither boy was particularly afraid. After the police left, Wolf and his friend found some adult escapees in the village, along with a guide. "During the night, suddenly when we moved around we could see that there were some other guys there who did the same thing. So, anyway, we attached ourselves to these people and we went across the border to the Western zone. When we came across the border we went into the English occupation zone, and the funny part of it is I hopped on the wrong train. I was totally tired, exhausted, and hopped on the wrong one, going in the wrong direction, and went to sleep."

He was 13 years old and heading north toward the Eastern zone, back to the Russians, when he'd wanted to go to his paternal grandmother's house in the Western sector in the French zone, where his mother was staying with his younger brothers. "So I hopped out wherever the next station was and went from there to the American zone, down to Alzey. Forget the hours, forget the no food, forget everything else, it was all traumatic and at midnight I ran into a French officer and he asked me where the hell I wanted to go. He spoke a little German and I mentioned this name,

Wolf as an apprentice in 1949.

Dautenheim, where my grandparents lived. Anyway, he drove me in his jeep up there."

Wolf's homecoming was not immediately welcoming. His brother Fritz remembers well when the doorbell rang that night. "First our grandma went out and she came back in. Mother asked who it was and grandma said, 'Oh, I think it was a little beggar who wants to have money and I was sending him away.' And our mother has an idea and asks grandma, 'Hey, how old was he?' Grandmother said the boy was about 14 and he had a black face. And mother said, 'Hang on, I will have a look.' She went to the door and we could hear her cry, 'Hey, it's Wolfie.' He was sitting on the stairs in front of the house."

Neither boy knew it then, but at his grandmother's house Wolfie was to taste for the first time the fruits that would influence the rest of his life. It was autumn and the grapes had been harvested and were in the cellar. Fritz recalls: "I went with Wolf in the cellar and he asked me, 'Fritz, what is this here?' And I told him, 'That's grapes and they taste wonderful.' And he said, 'Can I eat these Fritz?' And I said, 'Yes, you can but be careful, don't drink water later as you get bad diarrhoea. And he was eating, I think, two pounds of this and the next day he couldn't get up off the toilet. I told him, 'Wolf, I told you it is very dangerous.' He never was involved with wine before because he came from the Eastern sector and this was in the Rhineland." (The only

other vivid childhood memory Fritz has of his big brother is being saved from drowning by him in the River Ilm near their home when he was six.)

Wolf's mother returned to the Eastern sector with Wolf and his two brothers, where grandfather Otto was still there running the business in Stadilm, but not really in control. Later on it was confiscated by the communists. "My mother took me back, but not to the same school – that was out. And here the issue came again. I was another loose young boy on the street, so therefore my father, who was on the Western side, said, 'How about you come back across the border again? I have got a boarding school for you five kilometres out of Wolfsburg.'" It was winter and once again Wolf set off alone for the West.

"My mother drove me off with the car and said, 'You go across through this forest, on the other side is the American side.' Then I was stamping through this bloody two-metre snow, up the bloody hills, until I got to the other side, where with luck an American officer picked me up and took me up to a railway station and on I went to Wolfsburg, to the Heimschule boarding school in Burg-Neuhaus. How I paid for this journey I would not know. I may have had money in my pocket. My mother may have given me some West German marks or something, because the borders were closed by then and the East German mark was not worth a cracker, it was four or five to one west mark.

When he'd finished school, Wolf's father found him that first job with Edmund Diehl. "For me, that was probably the worst awakening, from being a free bird. I couldn't have found a worse person because he was building his company on cheap labour and was politically indoctrinated in what Nazism was all about. You know, people didn't mean anything to him." All the rage and fear that could reasonably be expected from the experiences of war are nothing compared to the lifelong bitterness Wolf harbours against Diehl. "He was a ruthless man, a dictator, a bastard, and the memory of him will always hound me."

The boy who had roamed free through the war and afterwards crossed borders and jumped coal trains to escape the discipline of a harsh boarding school now found himself in a place that was little better than a labour camp. Farm buildings were surrounded by a two-metre wall and permission was rarely given to leave the compound. Work was hard, with 11-hour days in summer when the light was long, seven days a week, and the pay was almost nothing. The tiny young apprentice cleaned the dairy and stables and fed the livestock before a breakfast of coffee, bread, honey and cheese. Then work would begin on the steep vineyards, weeding and cultivating the soil, spreading manure, all almost entirely by hand.

When there was no vineyard work, there were grain crops, beets and potatoes to tend and harvest. "At this time in my life there was only total confusion. There was no private life." All the farmhands, including the slightly built Wolf, wore yolks filled with grapes to be carried to the hand crusher. Because he was the smallest, and possibly because Diehl knew his father, he suffered less physical punishment than the other labourers, apart from being pushed around by Diehl and his sons. "I didn't gain very much knowledge here, except for bloody working. You never knew what job you were going to be doing from minute to minute. When it was raining, you

Division of Germany and Poland after World War II

East Germany

Berlin

West Germany

Poland

Czechoslovakia

Austria

Hungary

Wolf Blass (centre) with his brothers, Peter and Fritz. "For our parents and for us, for everybody involved, it was very, very difficult – to get separated all those years between East and West," Fritz says.

came back to the Eastern parts. I think in later years it was also dangerous to move over the green border, so he stayed in the Western part and I in the Eastern part. In 1952, we came for the first time, my mother, my brother Peter and me, from the Eastern part of Germany to Frankfurt. Our father found a little flat in Frankfurt and this was the first time we were all together since the war ended. Lots of German families were the same. For our parents and for us, for everybody involved, it was very, very difficult – to get separated all those years between East and West. You don't forget, never, never, never."

With food and accommodation in short supply for everyone, Wolf didn't tell his parents about the hard life at the Diehl farm. "I knew there was no way out of the system unless I could rescue myself."

had to hand-label the bottles and put them in cartons. The place was geared for the maximum use of labour."

Fritz remembers, when he was about eight years old, cycling five kilometres to visit Wolf on a Sunday in the township of Gau-Odernheim near the Diehl farm. "He told me, 'Hang on, Fritz, I don't have time for you, my boss is watching me. I have only perhaps 10 minutes time for you and then you have to leave me immediately.'

"I went back to the Eastern zone, to Thuringia, and Wolf finished his time at Diehl and he never

After a year at the Diehl farm, Wolf put an ad in a German wine journal seeking a wine and viticultural apprenticeship, counting the year at Diehl as the first of the required three years of training. This time he moved to one of Germany's leading wine regions, near the Bad Kreuznach area on the river Nahe, a tributary of the Rhine in the Rhineland-Palatinate in the northern part of the French-occupied zone. "It was still hard work, but it was in a civilised, good environment. There was no fear attached."

The days were still long, but Wolf remembers the farm owner as "good by nature, but a miserable man, mean with a lean personality". But there was freedom. "We boys, there were three apprentices, unknown to the family we collected eggs and wine to supplement the less-than-generous food supply. We became friends with the others from the working force who lived in the village and they were happy to get some of these eggs and wine. So we were alright. We had a hell of a good time playing sport and soccer and enjoying the pubs."

As an apprentice, Wolf learned every facet of the wine industry, including the processes for making every possible style of wine, even ice wine, when the grapes froze on the vine. He also did hand labelling, and watched and learned when auctioneers and buyers arrived to bargain. Twice a month, the apprentices attended classes at a research station to be tested on their understanding of the practical experiences they were having at the vineyard, a system that continues in Germany today.

By the time he'd finished his apprenticeship and received his Certificate of Viticulture, in 1952, aged 18, both Wolf's parents had been granted refugee status and were living in Frankfurt. His father had a job as a lawyer in the public service. Since the war had ended, when he was 11, Wolf had seen his mother and father only a few times. His first thought after completing his training was, "I am going to see my parents for a change."

In 1952, he applied for and got a job at Hans Schneider and Co in Frankfurt, where the learning that shaped his later successes undoubtedly continued. He remembers his boss, Hans Schneider, as "an entrepreneur, who had his business and underground cellars, and was a real estate agent and played on the stock market and with the horses".

It was also a wine distribution centre and this is where Wolf learned the blending skills that would eventually win him so many international awards and change the style of Australian wine. From his foreman, a veteran of the Eastern front named Knoll, he learned even more than winemaking techniques. And what Wolf learned is probably one reason he has made and kept so many friends from different stratas of society throughout his amazing life.

Knoll gave him the one thing he had never had – respect. And he taught him to respect others. "It was a wonderful experience for me to work with a person who actually explained constantly what life is all about. He always explained to me that the world is like a zoo and each animal is different. So each time we meet with somebody in a different category, we must treat them with respect. He made sure that down in the cellar, deep cellars that had been used during the war as a refuge from the bombing, that we occupied ourselves. We made brandy blends, did liqueur making, sugar conversions for the liqueur manufacturing side. We were washing bottles and storing them. We kept constantly moving, not hanging around smoking cigarettes and looking at each other, and I earned $1.25 an hour and I thought that was a great bloody income."

So here was Wolf, now 19 and full of knowledge about surviving in the big world. Then came another lesson, one he learned perhaps too well, if you ask some of the women in his life: the love of a woman, the boss's daughter, a 24-year-old divorcee he remembers chiefly as "very experienced".

In 1954, Wolf began studying for a diploma at the Wurzburg Wine University. He needed government assistance to pay the fees and this required an 80 per cent pass. It would be the first formal education to which Wolf had ever seriously applied himself. Within two years, he had passed every exam on wine processing with high distinctions and was the youngest person ever to receive the German Kellermeister Diploma. His reward for excellence was to be invited as a summer exchange student to the Champagne house of Pommeroy.

"My relationship with the French has never been any good. I haven't had too many good experiences and, then, also don't forget there has been definitely an animosity between the Germans and the French. Anyway, I didn't learn much. They had a very conservative approach to how they were handling the products – very secretly operated. They didn't have machines; it was the old hand paddle and everything else.

It was the real French Champenois process. When I came back, I thought to myself, 'No, that's not really my caper, I have to do something different.'" After a year with Hans Schneider, and despite the wisdom of Knoll and the charms of the boss's daughter, Wolf moved on to learn some more, this time as a wine expert at the Blumenthal Wine and Sparkling Wine Cellars at Linz on the River Rhine.

In 1956, he was appointed kellermeister for Karl Finkenauer in Bad Kreuznach. A family company, it had been established in 1828 and had an excellent reputation for the quality of its wines, thanks to a willingness to innovate as well as the terroir of the Nahe region, highly regarded, and which gave the Finkenauer wines great character.

Although he was to achieve fame initially in Australia as a red-winemaker, at Karl Finkenauer he built on his skills with white wine, as about 80 per cent of production was riesling from its own vineyards that won many awards at regional shows. Finkenauer also had excellent marketing and packaging, and was making and bottling dry, medium and sweet wines, grappa, non-alcoholic fruit juices as well as pioneering concentrated red-winemaking.

There could not have been a better place for a young kellermeister to learn every aspect of winemaking and the wine trade and, six years later, this experience would land him a job in Australia, which was at that time experiencing a boom in sparkling wine sales. The drinking habits of a nation that until then consumed beer, beer and more beer, with a little sherry or port for the ladies were changing.

In the meantime, for its new sparkling wine venture, Finkenauer had purchased the most modern machinery available, and it was young Wolf's job to bring it into production. "They came up and, bang, you know, we're building a big bloody hall. And then came the tanks and all the equipment and WB is scratching his head about how to do this stuff. I learnt quick smart." He had told the Finkenauers that, yes, he certainly knew something about tank fermentation because the university he had attended had a big wine farm. "But that was all hands off."

So when the company began buying the new equipment it was time for Wolf to do a crash course, so he contacted Germany's leading producer of sterile bottling equipment, Seitz, to work on the installation of the pressure tanks. The Seitz technician working with Wolf, once he recovered from his amazement that a 23 year old just out of university had been given such a huge responsibility, guided him through the process. Wolf buried his fear and grabbed the opportunity with all his heart and soul, although not without considerable apprehension. "I was in turmoil with myself, not knowing all the answers, but I had to perform."

Then there was the pasteurisation process to master. "Another thing which I had to learn, because I had never pasteurised the bloody stuff

in my bloody life. It had to be clean. We had to adjust the sugar levels and analysis. I had to do the laboratory work and everything else and all this type of thing. And then when you put the things on, where the vacuum is, you had to be careful that the vacuum didn't blow up the barrels. And I remember Mrs Finkenauer. She was absolutely delighted at the way we handled all the winemaking, the way the wines bloody won awards. And I think I gained a lot of respect, which was very important for me. I was very hungry to absorb things. I wanted to get ahead in life. I wanted to do things. One day, I told myself, things are going to be coming my way."

What came his way first was a man called Anton Massel, of Seitz, who had come to inspect the new plant at Finkenauer. Four weeks later, he offered Wolf a job as wine chemist at Copenhagen Wine Importers in London. Wolf had no idea then that this was his first step on the way to Australia. He had been having a wonderful time in Germany, driving between wine festivals at weekends with friends in his red Volkswagen,

By the time he'd finished his apprenticeship and received his Certificate of Viticulture, aged 18, both Wolf's parents had been granted refugee status and were living in Frankfurt. Wolf with (from left) Friedrich, Fritz, Irmgard and Peter.

visiting other friends in Frankfurt regularly, generally living life "flat to the board", working hard and playing just as hard. In fact, Wolf and his mates drank so hard, he says now that sometimes his car was almost going backwards, and indeed he survived a couple of serious car accidents without a scratch or a police record, according to brother Fritz.

When the London offer was accepted, the playing stopped. With typical thoroughness, Wolf started evening classes to improve his school English. He had no idea about the company he was to be working with, trusting that Anton had organised it and it would be well established. But it was a nightmare: there was no money for equipment, he couldn't afford decent accommodation and the bottling plant was controlled by a foreman who knew about spirits and whisky but not wine. His employer wanted to handle imports of German wine, sweet wine, already half fermented so that the bungs were flying off, and the losses were running into hundreds of thousands of pounds.

Wolf felt like he was facing professional disaster being associated with such a company, with no equipment apart from a secondhand filter bought from Germany. Unlike the state-of-the-art equipment he had been using in Germany, he now had to resort to using hydrochloric acid to sterilise the equipment. "The foreman nearly had a heart attack. He thought I was fucking

mad or something. But he was a Scotch man, he didn't know anything about wine." Wolf was devastated. He had taken this job because it was a chance to see a different country and to have a good time and he expected to be working in an established organisation, where he would be able to use all the knowledge and confidence gained at Finkenauer.

"Here again, this was an experience whereby I was put almost on the chopping block. It was unbelievable, what they were trying to do." Using sulphur to sterilise bottles in the underground tunnels where he worked, it soon became difficult to breathe. Fans had to be installed to clear the air. A sterile water system had to be devised to get the sulphur out of the bottles. "Everything had to be treated in a very, very primitive way. Anyway, we mastered this, we bottled the stuff, we kept things settled, we rearranged the transportation from the wine company and the English boss was never, ever sighted. He was sitting in London somewhere, typical English. And the only bloody way to talk to him was to telephone him."

In hindsight, the experience taught Wolf some valuable lessons about running a company; keeping a sharp eye on senior managers and staff and maintaining control of stock. In England, he became familiar with the habit of things having "fallen off the back of a truck". The pilfering was rampant and the insurance companies seemed not to care. "Whole containers of whisky or anything like this would just disappear. Or a

I was very hungry to absorb things. I wanted to get ahead in life. I wanted to do things.

WOLF BLASS

pallet of something or a half a pallet." Although Wolf shook his head in disbelief at the goings-on, he decided to not see what was going on, since almost everyone he worked with, including senior management, seemed to be involved. But he never forgot, and at his own company in Australia he instigated a strict regime of keeping track of stock. "That was a nightmare job at Copenhagen Wine, but the knowledge I gained helped me later on at Kaiser Stuhl [in Australia]."

Copenhagen Wine was importing and distributing sweet Liebfrau wine from Germany and sending it out in wooden casks, to Wolf's horror. "Today, you would get shot for doing that. It's totally irresponsible because you are contaminating everything that is in wood, which is contaminated to start off with. You would do it today in a stainless-steel container, with different anaerobic conditions and all that

stuff. I remember the Scottish foreman, he was bewildered – probably of my English – but we got on alright. He just couldn't understand what I was doing and I don't really know how he handled things before I came there. It must have been in chaos." Wolf arrived in time to deal with the second delivery to the plant. The first one had exploded.

In 1958, Anton Massel recommended him for a job as cellar superintendent for a much more professional and respected organisation, John Avery and Co in Bristol, on the River Avon in south-west England. His job was to control the huge amounts of wine, mainly red, arriving in wooden containers from Portugal, Germany and France. "Wooden containers meant oxidisation affected everything. Our job was to simply put things together, stabilise things, bottle it,

Wolf Blass in 1955, before he was appointed Kellermeister for Karl Finkenauer, where he learnt every aspect of winemaking and the wine trade.

label it, package and then distribute." For Wolf, Bristol was a milestone because, he says, it taught him how to handle people, including the English, who had to be "treated carefully because of my age and nationality … When because of my accent people thought I was from Rhodesia I let this go. I honestly did not blow the horn on that issue." Nor did he blow the horn when the war was mentioned. "You could have had an argument when the British showed you what happened in the war, where the bombs struck. You could have turned around and you could have said, 'You bastards, you bombed the bloody whole of Berlin.'"

Wolf concentrated instead on talking sport, nightclubbing with the hundreds of European au pairs who were then flocking to London, and improving his English by watching television. The brilliant television comedy of the 1950s and 1960s, *Hancock's Half Hour*, was instructional in the culture as well as the language. Wolf got every nuance in the stories of the grandiloquent, depressive, unemployed comedian Anthony Aloysius St John Hancock of 25 Railway Cuttings, East Cheam, and his mate Sid, a

working class conman played by Sid James. James was famous for his lecherous laugh and as the star of the highly politically incorrect and uproariously funny *Carry On* movies, where men – especially Sid in roles like Dr Nookey and Sir Sidney Ruff-Diamond – leered and women loved it. "They say Germans don't have a sense of humour, but I could bloody laugh my head off at the television, which was the first thing I had, a television to learn the language on."

Although perhaps he learned a little too much from Sid, if stories told by both the men and women friends he made during his first years in Australia – with great affection, it must be emphasised – are any indication. Wolf's second wife, Martine Barrie, says she changed Wolf when they married, counselling him about some of his "inappropriate" overt displays of affection toward the opposite sex. Martine says many of Wolf's old mates, male and female, never took to her. Perhaps merely because she was so much younger, at just 22. Or perhaps they regarded what she might call "inappropriate" behaviour as just another lovable sign of a man filled with an exuberance for life.

Despite the fact his nation had been at war with Britain, Wolf admired the working-class Brits. "That great sense of humour was a strength which I liked in them. They suffered during the war, too, you could see that. But there was a very old tradition, which had to be looked at with great respect. I might have had a title as manager, but I was not part of the owners with their big cars and lifestyle. There was a class distinction." Later, he was to find those same class divisions in the Australian wine industry. "The top people, the owners of the wineries, probably talked to each other, but down the ladder the winemakers were very much restricted. You know, if there's new machinery put up in a family-run company, they might invite the industry to have a look at it with a big fanfare. But you didn't learn anything. They were only showing how well off they were to be able buy this machine."

In Australia, alienated and overwhelmed by the potential for social embarrassment at the stuffy wine clubs the owners ran, Wolf gravitated to the small-business people, many in the distribution sector of the wine industry. "These guys, 80 per cent were either Italians or Greeks, they were new Australians who built their businesses. I found them easy to talk to because they wanted to learn. They wanted to make a dollar. They wanted to be somewhere."

Before he had given even a passing thought to Australia, however, his old friend Anton Massel bobbed up again with another job offer, this time in Venezuela. Around the same time he was also asked if he would like to go to Australia. "I thought Venezuela was a bloody marvellous idea. Being a bachelor, always believing South America is a hot climate and everything is cha cha cha." Then there was a revolution in Venezuela

before he could take up that offer. He visited Australia House in London, sampled their wines and decided, "I definitely can't go wrong here."

He returned home to farewell his mother, who cried. She said boys never came home. But Wolf had a guaranteed return airfare and definitely no plans to stay for life. Brother Fritz drove Wolf to the airport, in the 13-year-old Volkswagen that had taken him to so many parties and festivals, to catch his Qantas flight. Recalls Fritz: "Our mother, when she said goodbye to him, and we were waving to this Qantas airplane, it was the first 707, I remember, she said to me, 'I will never see Wolf again.' It was 1961 and she didn't know she would develop breast cancer, but perhaps it hurt her a little bit, but she never went to a doctor.

"Wolf was very generous, sending our parents two bills for a ship cruise from Genoa to Melbourne. It was in '64, but our mother was too ill to take this trip. He wouldn't have had much, but he was proud that he was able to send the money." Wolf didn't return to Germany until 1970. "After nine years, he came the first time to Germany and he could see our father alive. He died one year later. This time he was a very proud Australian citizen; I remember he was telling me, 'Everything here in Germany is awful. I never will come back to Germany.'"

But when Wolf had first arrived in Australia, at Darwin airport, his three-year contract suddenly seemed to him like a horribly long time. **W**

Chapter 3

INTO HELL AND HILLBILLY COUNTRY

The aircraft taxied to a standstill in front of a small tin shed. Wraiths of steam shimmered up from the tarmac toward the plane and its exhausted passengers. As the aircraft door opened, the tropical smells of rotting, over-ripe fruit and sweating humanity rolled into the tiny cabin. Wolf Blass, 27, recently of swinging sixties London and sophisticated Frankfurt, hesitated before stepping across the sweltering threshold into his new life in Australia. Perhaps he should have chosen the Venezuelan option, after all, lest, as his mother feared, he should vanish into the unfamiliar jungles of a country on the other side of the world. "I thought I had arrived in hell," he told ABC TV interviewer Peter Thomson nearly 50 years later of his first sight and smell of Australia from that aircraft on the tarmac at Darwin, Australia's northernmost capital, closer to South-East Asia than to any other Australian city.

When he had left Germany days earlier, it was 15 degrees below zero. Summer sits heavily on Darwin's shoulders and, in January, when Wolf arrived, it is suspended between the "build up", where skies are grey with low clouds that produce no rain but humid, damp air that clogs even your breathing, and "the Wet", when monsoonal rain cuts visibility to almost nil as it buckets down. These torrents are followed by brief dry periods, where the sun hits the fallen rain and turns it to steam. Like most European migrants who arrived in those days by air to Australia, Wolf would have spent up to 36 hours in a cramped, 90-passenger propellor jet

from London, stopping for refuelling in what today might sound like exotic locations – Rome, Cairo, Istanbul, New Delhi, Singapore. Back then, they were simply introductions to unfamiliar conditions in regions yet to transform themselves into the powerhouse economies of the 1970s and 1980s.

In later years, Wolf returned to Darwin often

> *I thought I had arrived in hell.*
>
> WOLF BLASS

as one of Australia's leading wine and horseracing identities to attend the Darwin race named after him. Back in 1961, the energy, determination and ambition to succeed that had seen him accept a winemaking job on the far side of the bottom end of the world carried him within days to places distinctively different in climate and attitude to devil-may-care tropical Darwin. He travelled to Sydney for three weeks to do promotional work and then on to Adelaide, the capital of the state of South Australia.

Back then, the so-called City of Churches had a reputation for public prudishness, but also an excellent food and wine culture far ahead of the rest of the country. Priding itself as untainted by convict settlers, Adelaide even today is often accused of having an entrenched conservatism running through its government and business. Certainly, that was the case when Wolf arrived. It is also a very isolated city: 3000 kilometres south from Darwin, where he had originally landed, 1000 kilometres from its nearest Australian state capital, Melbourne, 3000 kilometres from Perth in the west, 1400 kilometres from Sydney and 2000 kilometres from Brisbane. Swept by the Antarctic winds that cross the Great Southern Ocean and less than 1000 kilometres from the edges of the ancient deserts and saltpans of central and south-western Australia and the Northern Territory, it is just 60 kilometres south of the Barossa Valley, which was to become home to Wolf for the rest of his life.

In the beginning, however, it's doubtful that even Wolf would have imagined spending longer than his contract with Kaiser Stuhl in this most foreign of outposts. Because if Darwin had seemed like hell, the Barossa was like another planet. Hardly surprising, really, when you consider that it is only 800 kilometres (a day's drive to most Australians) from Coober Pedy, where residents build their homes underground to escape the heat and the pitted and scarred earth, denuded of colour and obvious plant life, has often been used as a location for adventure movies set on Mars.

A half-day drive from Kaiser Stuhl's Nuriootpa factory, where Wolf was working, is the Woomera prohibited area, where between 1952 and 1963 the British, with the support of successive Australian governments, carried out nuclear testing with a cavalier disregard for the human and environmental wellbeing of those who had called it home for tens of thousands of years. Consider this scant regard for the ancient spiritual significance of the place to the Pitjantjatjara and Yankunytjatjara Aboriginal people who were displaced by the Woomera test site, and it is hardly surprising that there was little knowledge of or respect, at the time, for any other culture, let alone that of a migrant who grew up in Nazi Germany. Wolf would have to integrate or leave.

World War II did ultimately breach the complacency of an isolated nation of 10 million people of almost entirely English heritage, living on the green edges of a tough, dry, empty continent, and Wolf was to play a huge role in changing the way Australians approached the good life, particularly as seen through a wine glass.

By the same token, Australia was to have a profound impact on Wolf. Two days after arriving in Adelaide, he was at the Angaston Country

Australia: comparative distances

Ball, about 20 kilometres from Tanunda, where he rented a room in the house of the local music teacher. At that first dance at Angaston, he could not quite believe such a society existed, although, as ever, he was ready to plunge into the thick of it. Peter Rosenberg, then a new neighbour and now one of Wolf's oldest friends in Australia, had been appointed as Wolf's "minder" to introduce him to the local scene. "Peter said to me, 'There's a big bloody ball, a big bloody dance up in Angaston! It's a little village further up.' I said, 'That's alright, I want to get into some action.'"

Peter collected him just after sunset in his FJ Holden, a 2.15-litre, six-cylinder, three-speed manual sedan that was even then an Aussie icon.

Wolf's friends Neil Tamke and Peter Rosenberg, 1973.

Its production between 1953 and 1956 marked a move by the nation away from a simple rural economy to a point where Australians realised, for the first time, that they could make and export something other than sheep, wheat and films about the Outback. At this time, wine exports were restricted to port and sherry. Nobody had yet considered exporting table wine as a profitable commercial venture. Not even Wolf.

At that first dance, he was interested in international exchanges of a different kind. In Bristol, he had lived in a penthouse apartment above the city's leading restaurant, Mauritania. "Of course, being in charge of a whole winery operation, I also made sure that I had a good relationship with the restaurateur. So you could take a partner and have a good time; you'd get there and think you had become part of the royal family. There was never a shortage of communication with people." In London, Bristol or other parts of the civilised western world, Wolf's communication was also easy, generally involving a few drinks shared with an attractive woman followed by the ultimate question of "Your place or mine?"

"Anyway, we went up to Angaston and Peter parked his car about 200 metres away from where all the action was and made a big entrance into the town hall. The first shock I had was all the girls sitting on the left-hand side and all the bloody blokes on the right-hand side! I was looking around, you know, inspecting what is available there, if there was anything there that would get my eyes into focus, and I said to Peter, 'To steady my nerves, how about we go into the bar and have a drink.' So he took me out back onto the street and we walked back to the car. He opened the boot, picked out a bloody bottle of beer and gave it to me."

A strange way to have a drink, but Peter explained it was illegal to drink at the dance, that all alcohol had to be consumed 200 metres from the premises. Later, Wolf learned more about the great divide between alcohol consumption and interaction with the opposite sex in Australia. "I thought it was hillbilly country. I honestly thought there was something wrong. Socially, we had a black-and-white television set, where women were sitting there indoors on the weekends and the men were sitting on the beer keg in the garage. And wine drinking didn't exist. There was only 1.5 litres of wine drunk for every 130 litres of beer, so that was a cultural shock to me."

But in the meantime Wolf had a lot more to learn that night at Angaston about the social interaction – or lack of it – between men and women in Australia. "So after we had a beer from the boot of the car, I went back and the music was playing. We picked up some good-looking birds and I did my usual talk, you know, asking where they were living and did they have a unit or flat, all this type of thing." As a social entry into a conservative society, it failed completely at one level. "I finished up running zero." But it was spectacularly successful in terms of getting Wolf noticed – a skill he honed to such a point that at one stage he was the best known and most famous winemaker in his adopted country. "I don't think it would have taken very long before people took some notice and said, 'What's the matter with this bloke?'"

He also met Bob Cundy that night at Angaston, the start of a lifelong friendship that saw them working together, at one stage literally tied like mules to barrows of concrete. "It was a good night, that dance. He was pretty lively and loved the women," recalls Bob. "There was plenty of excitement with him! He was, like, springing, you know, really lively and good company – very, very good company."

Elza Tamke also met Wolf in those early days, through her work at Kaiser Stuhl. Later she worked for him in the garage at his Nuriootpa home, hand-glueing labels on his first bottles of 1966 cabernet shiraz malbec, signed "Wolf Blass, Kellermeister Dip". Elza remembers Wolf's arrival in the Barossa Valley in 1961 as like a hurricane: "Oh my god! It was like we didn't know what hit the place."

It was the Germans, including many Lutherans fleeing religious persecution in Silesia and Prussia, who settled the Barossa, starting in the first half of the 19th century. They lived in appalling conditions – in hollowed-out tree

trunks, tents and mud huts – for years while they established farms and planted vines. They were stern religious folk and their grip on the culture of the Barossa is still strong in terms of food, wine and traditional festivals. But Wolf was part of a new wave of European settlers and Elza, too, was one of the "new" foreigners, arriving in 1949 from Latvia with her parents and six siblings at about age 8. With so few ties to the old establishment, apart from her husband, Neil, she accepted other

The British nuclear testing at Woomera, half a day's drive from Nuriootpa, where Wolf worked, was indicative of how this barren region and its people were regarded by the new White Australia.

newcomers with open arms, and Wolf was easy to like. "We did some crazy things. And, well, Wolf was a great one for taking his clothes off! And, oh, he was wild, his hands were everywhere. But, you know, it was just innocent fun and you could not help but like Wolf. He was a character. He was full of beans and always a laugh a minute. He has never forgotten his beginnings and especially the people that started out at the winery. They were always like a family to him and he has never, ever forgotten that. Today the wine business is just numbers for big companies but, I don't think Wolf would ever forget the people who helped him."

who would drop in for a meal or arrive with his children and a car filled with wine, saw a different side of the man she regards as an uncle. "It's strange, but I didn't feel comfortable seeing Wolf in all that glitz. I just don't think of him as a famous personality. To me, he looked wrong in those surroundings because he is just down to earth and has never had tickets on himself. He's just a genuine, nice fella."

At the Kaiser Stuhl Nuriootpa factory, Wolf was working for a company that had been established by growers who could not sell their grapes to the Valley's winemakers and wineries

You could not help but like Wolf.

ELZA TAMKE

There is a national belief – or myth – that Australia is the world's most egalitarian society. When a person becomes upwardly mobile from his working-class roots, his old friends will say he "has tickets" on himself. In 2004, Elza took her daughter Victoria to Wolf's 70th birthday extravaganza at the Hyatt Hotel in Adelaide, where his old Nuriootpa friends joined the city's social set. The younger woman, who had known him as a family friend of her parents, someone

during the Depression. Their answer was to form a co-operative to operate their own winery. Named after a flat-topped hill in the valley that reminded the early settlers of a place of the same name (Seat of Kings) in their homeland, the winery struggled with low prices and market instability and a reliance on exports, because Australians drank so very few table wines. World War II destroyed the export market and it was only in 1958 that the co-operative decided to introduce its brand to the still small Australian market, which had just embraced a completely new style of wine from the Orlando company, sparkling Barossa Pearl.

This was bubbly wine for the masses and the masses loved it, buying tens of millions of bottles. The winemaker and technical director of the South Australian Grapegrowers Co-operative, Ian Hickinbotham, had already changed the name on the co-op's labels to Kaiser Stuhl and had decided the next step to keep the business going was to follow Orlando into sparkling wine. After producing small amounts using secondhand brewery equipment and a secondhand filling machine from a mineral water company, he got bank financing and began producing a semi-sweet Sparkling Rhinegold under contract to Leo Buring. It was a huge success for the co-op and Leo Buring, and it gave the co-op the funds to expand and diversify.

And this is when he recruited Wolf Blass from the UK. Ian asked Wolf to check out the latest technical developments in Europe before he came to Australia. Wolf did this by signing up for a practical course at the Geisenheim Research Wine Technology University, then he worked for the sekt company Feist Sparkling Wine in Frankfurt, and at the automatic sterile bottling plant at Schade & Fuellgrabe, also in Frankfurt. He finished his preparation for his new job in Australia by working in the spirit treatment processing section of Hans Schneider & Co in Frankfurt. "What I didn't know was the financial and technical structure of my future employer in the Barossa Valley. From the questions they were asking, I expected to find highly technical facilities in production and bottling."

What Wolf found was a plant operating with a secondhand aerated water filter from a softdrink company, secondhand hermetically sealed retorts from a bankrupted local cannery, a separator on loan from Carlton United Brewery and a secondhand softdrink filling machine. He also found, in general manager Ian Hickinbotham, someone he considered a genius, leading a great think tank he created by employing practical people who could interpret his concepts.

"Today, nobody would believe you could build a fighting tank out of a sardine can, that you could redirect scrap into a production facility. If he [Hickinbotham] was a German they would have given him and his engineers a first class Iron Cross of Honour. There was a spirit of achievement and excitement to get things done under adverse conditions."

In a bid to diversify from its heavy reliance on bottling Sparkling Rhinegold for Buring, Ian wanted to launch Kaiser Stuhl's own line. It wasn't long before he and Wolf started Pineapple Pearl, in a pineapple-shaped bottle – and Wolf discovered his truly great talent for promotion. He suggested launching the wine by appearing to dispense it from a petrol pump. It wouldn't

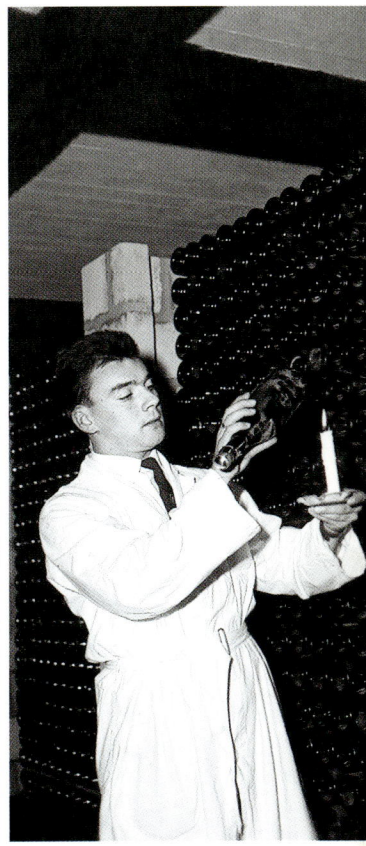

Wolf working as Sparkling Wines Manager at Kaiser Stuhl.

work with a sophisticated wine-drinking market, but for Australians in love with the new "pop" wine it garnered plenty of attention. Although the Pineapple Pearl failed to take off, within three years Kaiser Stuhl was making 80 per cent of all Australia's sparkling wine, albeit under contract.

Although his friends loved him, Wolf wasn't always popular with some of the employees at Kaiser Stuhl. "Their work ethics were about four out of 10. That's how co-operatives work. Laid back. She's alright, mate, she's alright. There was no free-enterprise pressure. If anybody didn't perform at least six hours out of nine or eight… you couldn't fire them, you could only make recommendations. Some of the guys at the co-op had just been there so long, and they were just moving at their own pace, which was a little bit of a cultural shock, but more or less only in this company. So my Germanic approach didn't go down very well with them."

By the time Wolf's three-year contract with Kaiser Stuhl expired in 1964, the company was producing a variety of wines never before – or possibly since – heard of. But they were feeding the new passion in Australia for any wine that bubbled. Labels included Yalumba Pearlette, Kaiser Pearl, Mardi Gras Pink Pearl, Tiffany, Sparkling April Gold, Sparkling Sangria, Sparkling Cold Duck, Cheo Frizzane (why should the rapidly growing Italian community in Australia miss out?), Clarevale Cooperative Sparkling Gold, Gala

Spumante and the aforementioned Pineapple Pearl and Cherry Pearl. As Wolf points out, these were frontrunners to the wine coolers of the 1980s.

By now, Wolf was hooked on the broader opportunities offered by the fledgling wine industry in Australia, deciding against other job offers, one at the wine research institute of the University of Southern California and two in Napier in New Zealand. Wolf certainly wasn't interested in living in California and, after a visit to New Zealand, dismissed it also as hillbilly country. "I don't think they exist any more, but at the time they had an apple-cider factory. To make wine and apple cider close by, can you imagine the problems you have got on the biological side? Yeast, bacteria, vinegar. You know, you get apple lactic/monolactic acid and all this type of stuff. So, anyway, that was too hot for me."

More than two decades later he would return to New Zealand in a joint-venture producing classic sauvignon blancs from the now world famous Marlborough region. But, in 1963, all he really knew was that he wanted to get out of an unhappy management situation at Kaiser Stuhl. Another flattering offer at that time came from Max Schubert at Penfolds, maker of the legendary Grange. Wolf didn't take it up, but it did lead him to a decision that would change the course of his life dramatically.

"Penfolds were looking for somebody and Max Schubert invited me to have an interview. But I would think because of my personality I

The Pineapple gift pack, from 1961. Although it ultimately failed, Wolf discovered his truly great talent for promotion.

Wolf Blass with Kaiser Stuhl wines, 1961. By the time Wolf's contract expired in 1964, the company was feeding the new passion in Australia for anything that bubbled.

Wolf and his famous blue Volkswagen Beetle, circa 1964, in which he covered tens of thousands of kilometres as a consultant. Wolf still owns a VW Beetle today.

when he joined, and when it was finalised Wolf got the opportunity that would set the Australian wine industry back on its stuffy establishment, not-very-high-quality heels. Wolf and Woodleys parted amicably, coming up with an arrangement that meant he was still blending for them on a freelance basis. This led to a suggestion from his friend, wine judge George Fairbrother, that Wolf concentrate on freelancing. "I said to myself, 'Freelancing, yeah, that's all right, probably eventually I can do my own wine on the side.'" The only other person to do such a thing was Leo Buring, in 1919, so it was a radical step.

Wolf bought a used blue Volkswagen and for the next few years covered tens of thousands of kilometres, earning a paltry $2.50 an hour, but consulting to a large number of clients, all of whom went on to become synonymous with good red wine. Yet Wolf was trained as a white-winemaker. His only experience with reds was in England when he supervised the blending of wines from Bordeaux and Burgundy for the venerable Avery's Wine Merchants (est 1793).

Wine writer Tony Baker describes Australian table wine produced in the early 1960s as "burnt and leathery". Writer, critic, winemaker and judge James Halliday says it "smelt and tasted more as if it had been baked than fermented". The exceptions were few and the greatest of them was the Grange Hermitage vintages made

wouldn't have fitted in and this is the reason why I didn't pursue the offer." Once his contract expired with Kaiser Stuhl, Wolf was bound not to make sparkling wines, pearl wines or champagne-style wines for three years. "They thought that I would detrimentally affect their business." They offered to pay his airfare to take the job in California. "I thought that if they are so bloody anxious to get rid of me, I must be good. I suddenly knew my place was in Australia." There followed a six-month stint as a blender with Woodleys, who made one of Australia's most famous sweet sherries, Three Roses, and the Queen Adelaide red-wine range as well as sparkling wine. But the sale of Woodleys was already being negotiated by Max Schubert, Australia's finest winemaker, according to Wolf and many others. But that was to change, dramatically, and by the mid-1970s Australians were tasting, spitting, sniffing and flocking to wine clubs and bottle shops for table wines. Wolf Blass, a German who trained as a white winemaker, was giving them a taste for consistent, quality red wine, as well as winning more awards than anyone in the history of the Australian industry.

Apart from Woodleys, however, Wolf's clients were struggling because they were small operations handed down from father to son, cultivating vineyards and making wine in the traditional ways of the family. They were relying on cellar-door sales, mail orders and some small private contracts to provide grapes. "There was no distribution, no marketing, no anything," recalls Wolf. With one of his most brilliant marketing moves – the relentless quest for medals – Wolf opened doors for them, supplying wines to the Wine Society in Sydney, a couple of big wholesalers and one of Melbourne's greatest restaurants, Massoni.

In his first year as a freelance winemaker for Normans, the company won Best Red Wine (claret) and Best Red Wine (burgundy), both made by Wolf, at the Royal Adelaide Wine Show. "So this rattled the business world." More medals came tumbling in for wines made by Wolf under the labels he worked for. Basedow took one of the most coveted wine awards in Australia, the Jimmy Watson trophy. "They all went up there and picked up the bloody trophies, while I did the dirty work in the rubber boots."

George Fairbrother worked for Robert Price and Sons, wine industry equipment suppliers, and he was also Australia's chief wine judge at all the national shows. Wolf recalls: "He told me what would be expected if you were going to put a wine into a competitive show. I knew that I used oak and I used different blending techniques, but the real crack of success came when I tackled the Langhorne's Creek wine district. This is where 80 per cent of the success came." **WB**

Wolf Blass at Kaiser Stuhl, 1961.

Chapter 4

AUSTRALIA'S COCKIEST WINEMAKER

Wolf Blass in 1963 with a farewell gift from Kaiser Stuhl. "I thought that if they are so bloody anxious to get rid of me, I must be good. I suddenly knew my place was in Australia."

Wolf Blass reckons he made Langhorne Creek. Equally, he says, Langhorne Creek made him. Its terroir, when combined with his blending skills, produced the wines that showed what a truly masterful winemaker he was. "It's the soil structure, the eucalyptus trees, the silt, the flooding from the Bremer River every year. I could see there was something in the flavour component unknown to all other wine districts I had been affiliated with." He spotted the region's potential working as a consultant for Bleasdale, when in 1965 the first of what would eventually be more than 3000 trophies and awards for Wolf's wines began rolling in.

At this stage, the awards went to his clients, starting with the gold for Normans at the Adelaide show. The first gold medal won under his own name, after he had established his business, Bilyara, in 1966, was the 1968 Wolf Blass Grey Label Cabernet Sauvignon Shiraz, from 100 per cent Langhorne Creek grapes. "It was magnificent, starting on your own and putting the first wine in a show and you are winning a gold medal."

It was also confirmation that he was right to believe that the grapes of Langhorne Creek would be the making of him. "I went all out in believing that the Langhorne Creek's fruit was going to get me where nobody or no other company had been, trying to source the fruit from there and develop a style of wine that was different. It differed from any other wine-growing region in

Australia and I had the proof of the pudding, because I had been there since 1964 when I was a consultant, getting around with my Volkswagen to Bleasdale Winery in Langhorne Creek to get this knowledge. I was convinced that their grapes were the best."

Wolf's next inspiration after deciding to use Langhorne Creek grapes was to make a softer style in order to introduce Australian women to reds. So while he had established his medal-winning formula of 70 per cent cabernet/30 per cent shiraz for his grey labels with Langhorne Creek grapes, there were other factors that went into the commercial success of all of his wines.

Mainly these had to do with Wolf's training as a white-winemaker and his eye for a new market. "I handled the red-winemaking in a delicate way, as you do white wine. It was more or less a white-wine-thinking brain behind how to make red. I changed the style. Drinkability, in my mind, became the key word and also the idea was to get women to enjoy drinking wine."

A key to achieving these goals was to get away from the heavy tannins that were such a feature of early Australian reds. "Wolf Blass' great contribution to the Australian wine industry stems from his belief that wine should be at its optimum from the day it is released," wine writer James Halliday says. "He was able to achieve that by sourcing most of his grapes from Langhorne Creek, which generally produces soft, fruity flavours well matched with the use of American oak." Wolf also considered other factors such as PH readings and acid-to-sugar ratios before grapes were picked. "Wine quality starts in the vineyard. Neglect this area and as a winemaker you have lost the race before it starts."

During harvesting, timing and speed are essential and double handling anathema. Any double handling at harvest can destroy colour and oxidisation will begin even before crushing starts. This is important because the phenols and tannins responsible for the wine's colour, astringency and pungency are all in the skin.

These are particular challenges in Australia, where temperatures range between 30C and 40C, increasing the risk of bacterial spoilage, oxidisation and hot fermentation. This is why Wolf insisted on mechanical harvesting in the cool of the nights, crushing in the vineyard itself, under refrigeration if possible, and immediate transfer by road tanker to the winery.

Probably the most significant difference in Wolf's winemaking compared with other winemakers in the 1960s was that every variety received every day from every grower at different times was kept separate and stored as different batches. "Instead, what the Australians had done, which is what most winemakers had done, was make the stuff and then put everything together, pressing, standing, first, second and third, pressing, put in the container, let it sit there and just wait for a couple of years before the wine was right.

It was more or less a white-wine-thinking brain

behind how to make red.

WOLF BLASS

I handled each individual batch in an entirely different process. Crushing different varieties and keeping them in the same fermentation vessel during vintage to achieve a combination of blends is senseless for the production of vintage, classic or individual wines. Each batch needs individual care from the moment it arrives until it is finally control-fermented and put in a container where it can rest and be evaluated. Early blending is of no use whatsoever."

Given this attention to detail at every stage, no wonder Wolf was offended when his competitors tried to put him down in the early days as "only a blender".

For many years, Wolf owned barely any vines, instead racing around the Barossa Valley to buy grapes from wherever he could find them for himself and his clients, and using their processing equipment rather than establishing his own plant. In fact, for many years he didn't own anything much but that very overworked Volkswagen and 1.6 hectares, which he planted out himself. In 1973, he continued to develop this land plot with help from good friend Bob Cundy, the longtime brandy maker at Tolleys. Bob recalls: "He came to me one day and he said, 'You come with me!' And we came out here to this area and there was this tin shed and he told me, 'I've bought that. I'm going to make a winery and you're going to help me.'"

The tin shed was initially built as a piggery and far from suitable. The first job was to build a concrete floor. Bob and Wolf spent every weekend for months digging out the dirt and moving it by the wheelbarrow load. Then Bob got his brothers-in-law, local builders, to bring in the concrete. But there were no roads into the shed and heavy rain had turned the soil into a quagmire, bogging the trucks. There was no choice but to go back to the wheelbarrow.

"We had to have a rope on the front and one of us pulled and the other one pushed," laughs Bob. "This is the way Wolf and I used to pull

At the Horse and Herring Club in the 1990s. "It was about the handshake and understanding what you were doing. You'd have some wine, become jovial and not really worry about things."

it through the mud and stuff. We did half of the little building one weekend and the next weekend we did the other one."

With the piggery/winery sorted, the next important building works to be completed were the entertainment room, dubbed the Horse Bar, and a barbecue. Later it would become the venue for the Horse and Herring Club, something Wolf had started at Kaiser Stuhl to bring different people from the industry together socially, a way of doing business that died with the takeovers and acquisitions of the 1980s and 1990s.

"Before that happened, people didn't sit in these bloody square boxes. It was about the handshake and understanding what you were doing. You'd get drunk and you didn't really worry about things and you had friends in the Police Commission and everything else. That

was the club whereby I got outside winemakers to come in with their products on a Friday night and congregate, having a marvellous bloody time," Wolf says.

Ian Hickinbotham and the artist and label designer Neil Tamke were founding members, and since there wasn't much in the way of delicatessen food available in those days they'd buy tinned herrings and biscuits to go with the wines. "It was a turning point of getting other wine companies and their staff involved socially amongst each other." They also studied the form for the next day's horseracing and made their bets, hence the horse part of the title.

But before the Horse and Herring Club was up and running at Bilyara, and after 25 years at Tolleys, Bob Cundy had a big decision to make. Wolf asked him to come work fulltime with him.

FROM STRENGTH TO STRENGTH

1973-1976 W.F.O. Blass Bilyara Vineyards

1977 Wolf Blass Wines Pty Ltd

1978-1983 Wolf Blass Wines International Pty Ltd

Year	Net Assets $	Vintage Stock $	Containers (Barrels & S/s Tanks) $	Plant & Machinery $	Winery & Property $	Cash & Debtors $	Creditors, Leases & Loans $
1973	177,300	142,700	16,200	7600	10,000	24,100	38,800
1974	358,700	273,300	41,700	9500	46,600	52,300	64,700
1975	623,900	495,500	59,300	41,000	89,000	26,000	32,000
1976	1,026,400	690,000	87,100	32,800	151,000	70,000	117,700
1977	1,403,900	1,158,000	123,600	36,000	200,000	52,000	191,600
1978	1,821,600	1,387,000	155,000	53,700	230,000	225,000	291,000
1979	3,080,500	2,163,000	252,000	86,000	514,000	470,000	584,000
1980	4,587,300	3,717,000	478,000	99,000	694,000	430,000	1,135,000
1981	8,468,400	7,007,000	753,000	219,000	1,132,000	859,000	1,820,000
1982	11,449,000	9,910,000	820,000	248,000	1,793,000	1,500,000	2,977,000
1983	14,102,200	12,324,000	1,029,000	321,000	1,906,000	2,180,000	3,806,000
1984	15,880,500						

March 1984 New Company floated

May 1984 Prospectus for Wolf Blass Wines issued

June 30, 1984 Prospectus oversubscribed

    31,400,000 Capital 50c shares

    18,839,434 shares = Wolf Blass 60%

    12,560,566 shares = Public 40%

November 7, 1984 Inaugural AGM held at Wolf Blass Winery, Nuriootpa

Directors

Wolf Blass, *Managing Director*

Ian Edgeley, *Chairman*

Bob May, *Director & Secretary*

At that time, Bob was raising a large family and it was a big step to leave secure employment with a well-established company to work for a small winemaker with a converted piggery, a registered company name, a huge talent for winemaking and marketing and not much else other than enthusiasm for the future.

Says Bob: "He was the best boss I ever worked for! The reason? You worked, he paid! For the first three years there was no five-day week, no eight hours a day. And this definitely put me on my feet and he gave me some opportunities."

In 1966, Wolf had registered the name Bilyara after he realised there was an existing winery using the same name that belonged to a group of growers he felt had treated him unscrupulously. After enjoying his little payback moment, with typical thoroughness Wolf asked Adelaide University the meaning of the word. The answer, that it was Aboriginal for eagle hawk, convinced him fate was on his side and urging him forward. "Being German, of course, the eagle was very appropriate. So the name was really symbolic of both my German and Australian connections."

The way the name and label developed were also symptomatic of Wolf's own path to the top of the wine industry. "It's a bit of a Walt Disney fantasy the way we have achieved what we have today. After the war, there was no industry, no commerce in Germany, total chaos, so there was no other objective for me other than going on to a wine farm, where I am going to get some food, some work and a bed to sleep in! This is the way I slipped into the viticulture and wine industry – not by choice, but by necessity."

The next Walt Disney moment arrived just before the 1973 vintage. Since 1969, Wolf had been manager and winemaker for United Distillers, trading as Tolleys, a company best known as a brandy producer. Within three years, Tolleys had been turned into one of the most successful red-wine exhibitors in Australia. But the board objected to Wolf continuing to make his own wines. He said he was determined to continue with his winemaking and, with the help of a lot of loyal friends, that is how the tiny Bilyara of 1966 became Wolf Blass Wines International in 1973.

In 1984, it became a public company with market capitalisation of $15.2 million. By 1991, following a merger with Mildara, Wolf was deputy chairman and a major shareholder in Mildara Blass Limited with a market capitalisation of $125 million. The chart on page 57 shows just how phenomenal the growth of Wolf Blass wines was in the 11 years to 1984. In 1996, with his children not interested in following Wolf into the industry, Mildara Blass was acquired by Foster's for $560 million.

But on the day that Tolleys told him to choose between making his own wines or staying with them, none of this could have been anticipated

Wolf Blass in 1962, a man who drums to his own tune, often on a handy table or bar.

even in Wolf's wildest dreams. "They asked me if I am going to carry on my little production. Or am I going to work 100 per cent for them? I had a couple of telephone calls and in a particularly Australian way I used the two fingers and said, 'You can stick it!' And I walked out of the boardroom and that was the end of the affiliation. And I started my own company with a $2000 overdraft."

He had no experience in running a business. "But I knew that hard work is going to get you there and I also had a very strong, friendly relationship with the companies I had been working with as a consultant. They helped me along to start off becoming an independent person within a couple of years."

So typical of the way Wolf never loses touch with the people who have been important in his life, he called his by now estranged first wife, Raelene, to discuss whether to leave Tolleys and go out on his own. The pair had met on a blind date in Nuriootpa in 1965, married in 1967, had two daughters and separated in 1971.

"He was a handful, a big handful. A lot of

times I could control it and go along with it, but there were times when I couldn't. But, yeah, I don't regret the times with him," Raelene says. "He would say it himself: he was a bit of a ladies' man – a big bit – and this was part of the problem."

Not that she ever had any doubts about Wolf's ability to be a success at anything he chose to do in his business life.

So when he telephoned to ask whether he should leave Tolleys, she told him he should, knowing this would be his decision, anyway, once he'd talked it over. "There was no way he was ever going to go backwards. He's his own best PR. He's got a brain like I wish I had and he deserves everything he's got. He had a few conflicts with Tolleys, but he would never admit that some of it was him. He had the choice of staying where he was, doing his own thing or doing it for them. He was beating them in competitions and wine shows. Of course, there had to be conflict, I mean, they couldn't have an employee that was beating them at their own game."

When he left Tolleys, Wolf wasn't starting completely from scratch. In 1967, he already had 1500 cartons of his own wine and by 1968 and 1969 he made more. "So I was therefore in my own right, on stockholding, quite a wealthy fellow." But he had no cash flow. If he was to sell the wine he needed licensed

Quelltaler Estate in the Clare Valley, with 137 hectares of vineyards amid historical stone cellars, was renamed Eaglehawk Estate.

My wines are not big, like some you can stand a teaspoon in. Our success is to make delicate wines with heavy oak penetration.

premises. That's when he turned to his mate and SP bookmaker Norton Schluter at the Greenock Creek Tavern on the edge of the Barossa. Norton met Wolf very soon after his arrival in Australia. "This little German fellow popped up in our bar here, where we had an SP bookmaker operating, and he was wanting to bet on a racehorse. To get some German guy just arrived out here to pop over on a Saturday afternoon to have a bet was most unusual. Actually, it turned out that it's a part of Wolf's character, because to my mind you don't get people immigrating that adopt the Australian way of life so quickly as he did. Because he really did almost everything, you know, he adopted our way of life immediately."

Norton had always sold quality aged wines, although at that stage he would not have considered Wolf, the maker of sparkling "pop",

as a potential source. "I used to buy what I thought was the top quality wine. I'd buy Peter Lehmann, I'd buy Bleasdale and a few Yalumba signatures and that sort of thing and put them down here, and cellar them for a couple of years and then bring them out after the wineries had virtually sold out of that particular vintage. And it turned out to be quite good for me because in those days they made wine that required bottle age."

When Wolf came along with the then revolutionary idea that you could buy a wine and drink it immediately rather than needing to cellar it, Norton was quick to buy from him, and Wolf was typically generous to a mate. "He was always good to me because he gave me a very good quota of his own grey labels and yellows, even though he wasn't making a lot of wine in those days. Then he started winning all those

Wolf Blass 'Silk Gloss' advertising, which symbolised a combination of power and elegance.

gold medals and he had Neil Tamke putting them on his labels, which most of the others never did. So they started saying he wasn't a good winemaker he was just a blender, which was complete rubbish."

His competitors also said Wolf's wine wouldn't last. At first Wolf was too busy making his mark on the market and winning more medals to address that particular slur. But, of course, it was an insult he would not forget, and one that he was to challenge in his usual, spectacular fashion, organising what is recognised even decades later as one of Australia's greatest wine tastings, assembling Australia's high priests of the palate.

But first he had some marketing to do, and the best way to do that was to turn himself and his own larger-than-life character into a media darling.

While the big companies such as Yalumba, McWilliam's, Tyrrell's, Houghtons and Rothbury Estate had sales forces and their own distribution network, the small ones like Wolf had no way of getting the attention of the wine wholesalers and drinkers except through publicity and the cachet of medals that would make people go out of their way to find and try their wines.

In an industry that was clubby, stuffy and conservative, he began actively chasing publicity, starting with trade papers and magazines that were read by retailers and distributors and most

people involved in the industry. This would evolve over the years to reams of newspaper and magazine articles and hours of television interviews on shows that would these days go under the title "lifestyle".

And then there was the gossipy magazine *The Entertainer*, launched in 1983 with a dinner at one of Melbourne's leading restaurants, Alexander's, produced by Wolf Blass Wines and inserted into the leading gourmet magazines in Australia, the UK and Japan, as well as in the in-flight magazines of the two major Australian domestic airlines of the time, Ansett and Qantas.

Success in expanding the customer base also gave Wolf an unexpected confidence boost. He began to see himself not just as a great winemaker, but as a businessman. "I was the guy who actually made it and was successful in wine shows, so people started contacting me. If I hadn't been successful in wine shows, I wouldn't be sitting here today. It is a little bit of a miracle, if you ask me, but I had to do something different in order to succeed. Because, as a totally independent person against family concerns which had been established for over 100 years, I had to do something different and I think I succeeded."

Certainly, the media began to pay attention and the adjectives flowed faster than a chilled white on a hot Barossa day. As wine writers, columnists and journalists were exposed to the Wolf charm offensive, trawling their thesauruses

The eagle was very appropriate ... really symbolic of my German and Australian connections.

WOLF BLASS

they delivered superlatives about the man and his brand such as determined, argumentative, cheerful, ebullient, opinionated, assertive, idealistic, irrepressible, effervescent, wicked, twinkling, extroverted, personable, acidic, shrewd, vital, emotional, astute, egotistical, purposeful, womanising, generous, volatile, sensitive and irrepressibly voluble, among others. He was labelled "Australia's cockiest winemaker."

Writer Tony Baker called him Germany's most successful export to Australia since metwurst. Some even dubbed his wines Son of Grange, a reference to the benchmark Grange Hermitage.

As Wolf puts it, bluntly: "My wines are not big, like some you can stand a teaspoon in. Our success is to make delicate wines with heavy oak penetration. Oak and fruit, that's where Max Schubert made his success with Grange Hermitage".

When he finally began winning awards in Australia, Wolf was in no mood to take a conciliatory stance on how long it had taken him to get noticed. "Our style hasn't changed since I first made dry reds after leaving Kaiser Stuhl. It took the judges five years to recognise the wine I made."

But he admits, "Winemaking doesn't make me tired, but the selling, the promotion, the advertising does."

By 1973, Wolf had made his mark on Australia's wine industry, but he was exhausted, emotionally and physically. By 1974, however, he was on top of the world. **WB**

Wolf's mates (from left): Stan Gillman, Jim Smythe and Brian Linke.

Wolf's personal friend and GP, Dr Michael Hawkes, with his wife, Merridy.

Wolf with Bill Potts (left) and Len Potts from Potts Langhorne Creek, 1997.

Wolf with Rainer Schwind, formerly of Pieroth Wines.

Chapter 5

A YEAR OF JOY

Above: The first winemaker to win four of the coveted Jimmy Watson Trophies, in 1973, 1974, 1975 and 1998.

Always ahead of his time, Wolf was criticised when he started winning all those gold medals and had Neil Tamke put them on the labels.

The first big success that was to put Wolf on the path to multimillionaire and wine legend status was in 1974 – he calls it his Year of Joy. "That was one year, if I would have jumped out of the Hilton Hotel, I would have fallen on two feet without breaking a bone! Everything was going right; the Jimmy Watson, the packaging awards, connection with the distribution network, and it was just a year of full joy that everything was falling into line."

The Jimmy Watson Trophy, named after a famous bar owner and wine enthusiast in Melbourne, is the Australian wine industry's most coveted trophy, awarded annually since 1962 for the best one-year-old red. Wolf Blass Wines won it an unprecedented three years in a row, something no winemaker has done since. Another record was set when the 1998 Wolf Blass Black Label also won the Jimmy Watson – making the tally four. The only other wines to have won the Jimmy Watson Trophy more than once are Penfolds Grange, Cape Mentelle Cabernet Sauvignon and Katnook Cabernet Sauvignon.

But in late 1973, the final breakdown of Wolf's marriage to Raelene and the decision to leave Tolleys and start a new business almost killed him. "I took everything on my chin and handled it all, but I suppose the body can only take so much." He had always been a heavy smoker, getting through 10 or 12 cigars or cigarellos a day, remarkably without affecting his palate. In September 1973, he was admitted to the Lyell McEwin Hospital in Elizabeth, an Adelaide suburb, for a week

This newspaper cartoon by Norm Mitchell added fuel to the fire after Wolf's speech accepting the Jimmy Watson upset the establishment. "The publicity was bloody tremendous – there was no doubt about this. Just because of the statement I made."

I TOLD YOU MY WINES WERE SEXY !!

WOLF BLASS WINES · BAREFOOT CRUSHING DEPT · DER GOLD MEDALS

of tests for suspected angina. It turned out instead to be total exhaustion. Wolf was fortunate enough to get a doctor who understood the nature of his driven patient, unlikely to heed advice unless scared into changing his ways.

"My smart doctor, a Malaysian doctor, was a wonderful man. He showed me a false X-ray and he explained to me that my lungs were very much affected because of the heavy smokes and he frightened the life out of me." Wolf has not smoked since, but it took several weeks to cope with the heavy withdrawal symptoms and he was a nervous wreck. He also had high cholesterol and high blood pressure. "From that day onwards I have been on a cholesterol diet and I have never touched a cigarette and I have been galloping along without any real health problems ever since."

Wolf also buried his personal pain over the marriage breakdown by working obsessively. "In some way it took some mental setbacks like this

for me to realise that I had so much in front of me to achieve and to make a success, which was an obsession with me. I think this is probably a message to anybody that, if things are going to go wrong outside your own doing, the best way is for you to keep working in order to dilute what otherwise could become a nightmare."

(Mind you, this same work ethic also contributed to the breakdown of his second marriage, to Martine Barrie, in 1980. She was 24, he was 44 when they wed. "I didn't have the maturity to comprehend the mission that man was on," Martine says. "I misconstrued: I saw that he did not love me, adore me, see me as the sunshine in his life, as number one. I felt very much secondary. Had I had a greater maturity or concept of the journey he was on, I wouldn't have taken that quite so personally.")

In his 1974 Year of Joy, however, Martine was still at school and Wolf's thoughts were definitely not on marriages past or future. He was at the Friday luncheon at Greenock Creek Tavern when Bob Cundy rang him to say the Melbourne Show Society wanted samples of his entry sent to them for public tastings. A sure sign, although not official confirmation, that he'd won the Jimmy Watson. Wolf took the call and his fellow lunchers noticed he was unusually quiet for the rest of the lunch. "They knew something was going on, but you're not supposed to say anything at this stage and I think I looked more shocked than pleased. I

My wines are sexy, they make weak men strong

and strong women weak.

WOLF BLASS

went back to Bob at the winery and talked about it and then I think I hit the bottle."

Despite his successes, Wolf has always felt the country's winemakers take something of a risk in entering shows, because not winning is a great defeat in the eyes of the public. "But winning is definitely a leverage for a good commercial start, good selling, good promotion, good image, good everything." He certainly leveraged the win into instant publicity, declaring in his acceptance speech that "my wines are sexy, they make weak men strong and strong women weak". It "blew the top off" the conservative Royal Melbourne Wine Show.

"The publicity was bloody tremendous – there was no doubt about this. Just because of the statement that I made. And then we celebrated. We went to the Jimmy Watson Hotel in Carlton and, you know, whatever money I had, that was definitely splashed and handed out at the door, because everybody is turning up there and trying to celebrate with you. The camaraderie isn't there

within the wine industry anymore. But, then, you invited all your mates, they all came from all over the place and it was always into the Jimmy Watson."

By the time he won the third Jimmy Watson, in 1976, Wolf estimated the award had been worth at least $1 million in publicity alone. This in turn gave him a "comfort zone" with banks, which he didn't need, anyway, thanks to his reluctance to go into debt unless absolutely necessary. "Also, it was a stage whereby people who have been dealing with me from the grape-growing industry and from other wine-supplying companies knew that, if they dealt with us, they are safe, that they are getting their money. It definitely would have put the name Wolf Blass on the market."

Builder and friend John Gordon vividly recalls Wolf's reaction to winning that third Jimmy Watson. "We were in the Greenock Tavern for the Friday lunch club and Wolf said there would be a phone call if he had been successful. The phone call came and he went out to the front bar.

He was out there for about five minutes and I went to get him and he was laying on the counter hyperventilating. He couldn't breath."

His first three years of business had been one of such incredible expansion that it still almost takes Wolf's breath away when he looks back. "I actually had a business. I couldn't quite understand all of this, because we were bloody everywhere. I had half a million dollars worth of vintage stocks in there, three times what I started with in '73. So I could see that I had the labels in place, I had the packaging in place, I had the marketing in place and I was selling it. I was in full flight – '73, '74, '75!"

But he didn't even have a building in which to store his stock. "I was selling from different places, where I had my stock placed. The wines were bottled, then stuck in McLaren Vale with one company and Clare in a different company."

The first step to remedy this situation was to tear out almost all the vines he had planted around the piggery/winery to make way for expansion, leaving him with a token planting over about 0.4 of a hectare. He had no grapes, no vines and no plant or equipment other than oak casks and stainless-steel tanks. The decision not to own vineyards was well ahead of its time, with others not taking this route for decades. Until 1984, when he bought the Australian Bottling Company, Wolf did not even invest in a bottling plant, preferring to take a share in someone else's and become the primary customer. Rather than grow his own grapes, he

went to vineyards and offered to buy at the best price. He had no big, expensive crushing facility, preferring to do business with existing owners.

"He was very, very good in the way that he set his structure up, considering business wasn't his strength," Bob May recalls. Because Bob joined Wolf in those early years, he has probably been closer to him in terms of knowledge of the business than anyone. "Wolf, despite his outside flamboyance, was an extremely conservative individual and that's where we both worked well together, because I was a conservative non-risk taker. His conservative nature worked with mine and between the two of us we basically ran things through. He could add the figures up and he had that streetwise ability – or cunning – and he was very good and quick with numbers. He could see the picture very quickly."

Wolf's major investment was in oak casks, which he would write off in the first year as an operational cost and expect to get five years use out of. "Our biggest expense was the sheds that housed the oak and they were just big warehouses with oak and oak and oak and oak. And they just kept growing and growing and growing," Bob says. "He had a plan in front of him where he was going to grow. He had this confidence in his own ability to sell his product and had the plan for where the next shed was going to go and the next and the next, all planned 10 years in advance."

Because Wolf was always prepared to send himself up if it helped to sell his wine – to make controversial statements, stage headline-grabbing events and sell, sell, sell himself outrageously if necessary in the interests of marketing – many people put him down as a lightweight in business terms. Bob continues: "He had a master plan and again that's where a lot of people didn't give him credit. They said he was just a blender of wine, he was just able to get this and get that and market it. But it was these other abilities that he had behind him that made him successful. Sure, he had someone like me alongside of him, but it came from him to have his capital outside of the vineyard. It caused us difficulties later on when there was a grape shortage, but in those early years it really enabled us to grow unbelievably rapidly." In the end they had to buy vineyards. "But he fought me. He always said, 'I hate the bastards, Bob, I can't buy bloody vineyards!' And he'd fight me. But in the end we had to buy some vineyards."

Although he didn't want to own vineyards, Wolf spent a lot of time in the early 1970s dealing with them. "I almost became a moving vehicle, I was constantly on the move to find out 'Where can I

get wine?' because I needed the supply system." But it was never just about the money.

Even after Foster's acquired Mildara Blass in 1996 and Wolf embarked on a successful career investing in the stockmarket and property, his needs remained simple, according to Bob May: "The money was always incidental. He'd be happy with just a comfortable little home. As long as he's got his Mercedes and he can go to the footy with the blokes and his mates, he's happy."

Bob is one of a large group of lifelong friends who contributed to the Wolf Blass success story

Longstanding Wolf Blass friend and entrepeneur, John Gordon, with his wife Ruth.

by being strong enough to stand up to him yet open minded enough to like and respect him, despite his difficult and often dictatorial nature. They were also wise enough to understand that beneath the brusque exterior and the self promotion is a man of boundless enthusiasm who not only needs friendship, but also repays it over and over with loyalty.

In the 1970s, while Wolf tore about the Barossa with typical tunnel vision, his mates stepped in to provide him with some tangible signs of success, something to show for all that running around apart from awards, booming sales and the buzz of growing a great business. They began by looking at his headquarters and decided something had to be done. Here was their mate, jetting off to Hong Kong to set up an export business, winning more awards than anyone had ever done before, and yet he was working out of a place that looked more like a neglected farm than the HQ of a leading winemaker. John Gordon offered to build him a garden. "All he had was a chook shed out the front." John drew some sketches but Wolf, in typical blunt fashion, pronounced his ideas as "shithouse".

Winemaker John Glaetzer knew how to deal with that kind of reaction from his mercurial employer. He'd already had to deal with the

The Board of Directors

WOLF BLASS
Managing Director
Married with two daughters
Resides in Barossa Valley

IAN EDGELEY
Solicitor, LL.B., 13 years and Partner with a Law firm for 10 years
Associate Director and Chairman of Wolf Blass Wines and associated with Wolf Blass as legal adviser since 1974
Aged 34 years, married with two daughters
Resides in Adelaide

JOHN GLAETZER
Director of Operations
Oenologist Graduate, Roseworthy College
32 years of age, married with two daughters
Associated with Wolf Blass since 1970
Resides in the Barossa Valley

MICHAEL FALLON
General Manager
Associate Director
Associated with the liquor industry since 1968 through Burns Philp. In 1977 Michael became involved with Wolf Blass Wines for the first time on a professional basis.
38 years of age, married with three children
Resides in the Barossa Valley

BOB MAY
Chartered Accountant F.C.A and Secretary of Wolf Blass Wines since 1975
Associate Director and Partner in an Accounting firm for 10 years
34 years of age, married with two children
Resides in Adelaide

first shed in which Wolf and Bob Cundy had built the floor by the wheelbarrow load. "Everyone had told him, 'Wolfie, pick the shed up, lift it up.' He'd built it too low and no money could lift it, it was a bloody nightmare from day one and one room kept flooding." But it was difficult to get Wolf to sit down and agree to plans for new buildings, because he simply could not or would not take the time to read and understand drawings. Glaetzer solved the problem by physically moving Wolf's office furniture outside into the dirt paddock. "I'd get the spray paint out and paint the walls around him and then he would be happy."

So when John Gordon's garden plans were given the knock back, John Glaetzer took over. "Johnny Glaetzer and I ganged up on him," John Gordon recalls. "We knew when he was leaving for Hong Kong so we got some pigface from down Langhorne's Creek, a lot of plants, trees, shrubs and a great big oval vat where we put a motor inside the pump and ran red wine (it was really coloured water) through it and through a little waterfall down through the garden. Then we got pavers in to pave it, and Wolf got back off his trip and he came along and he said, 'That's not the bloody sketch you did.' And I said, 'Yes it is.' And he was thrilled. We hadn't quite finished it, so he got out there with a spade, but all he did was lean on the spade. So that was his little garden. That won, I reckon, three or four awards."

This was just one example of the many times Wolf's down-to-earth Australian mates dealt with his nature – the little dictator of Stadtilm, Germany, had met his match in the gruff, no-nonsense tradesmen (and they all were men) who befriended him when he arrived in the Barossa Valley. It was the same with Wolf's boating.

Wolf bought a boat called *Duplex 2* with John Gordon and, once again, Wolf took on the role of the leader, never mind that he knew next to nothing about boats. The friends made many trips together to nearby Kangaroo Island, often taking along Wolf's daughters, Sharyn and Susan, who spent weekends and holidays with their father after he and Raelene separated.

Looking back, John Gordon says he can't believe he ever let Wolf take the boat out on his own, given his willingness to tackle any challenge regardless of his monumental ignorance of basic boating safety. "How he ever got home sometimes, I'll never know. We were on one trip fishing and we were going into Christmas Cove and there were a few little rocks about and, of course, we go in there, the wind swirls around and there's a big cliff around it where you get into Penneshaw, where you get off the ferry there. There's a boat mooring there and you come in with both your motors to the moorings straight up the end.

"Wolf's yelling, 'Slow down, slow down!' And I eased the boat up to the wharf and I said to my mate who had come out with us, 'Leave it to Wolf, he knows all about boats.' And we stepped off and said, 'It's all yours, Wolf!' It took him two hours to untangle all the ropes he had tangled himself in and he came up to the pub and he wouldn't bloody speak to me. But it doesn't last long with him, unless it was something against him personally. He saw the funny side the next day!"

John Gordon recalls also how Wolf's passion for boating nearly ended his brilliant career before it began. "His boat was a 28- or 24-footer, but Wolf could get bloody lost on it. He came back one day and said he couldn't find where he was going, and he'd had to anchor up and get rescued. Turns out he had the compass sitting on top of the bloody motor and the compass was going around the same revs as the motor."

Another time, he and Wolf, with their daughters, were fishing about eight kilometres off Kangaroo Island when Wolf decided to stop the boat on the top of a wave. "Oh, it'll be all right, Cookie" was Wolf's response to Gordon's frantic cries as the girls turned seasick green and the exhaust fumes poured into the boat. This was a petrol boat – the one blend Wolf should never have been allowed within 100 kilometres of. He certainly should not have been allowed to fuel up. He did, of course, and on the day when the cap came off the reserve tank he almost took himself, several people and some nearby buildings with him into the heavens.

"There was that much bloody petrol floating around the bilge and a red-hot motor and a newspaper writer on board who smoked like a train, and Wolfie had already pumped 40 gallons into a 20-gallon tank when this bloke asked how much the tank could hold, and then they noticed the cabin was flooded with petrol." His mates laugh later that Wolf ran from the boat at such speed, his feet didn't touch the ground till he was 150 metres away. John Gordon told him, "Wolfie, you are going to kill yourself on that thing." Wolf sold the boat and two months later it burned to the waterline under the new owner.

Likewise, Wolf's passion for cars and his enthusiasm for getting involved in every community sporting club also causes a lot of affectionate hilarity among his mates, even now when they recall some of his eccentricities and his competitiveness. When John Glaetzer bought a souped-up Ford Fairlane with a sunroof, Wolf just had to have a sun roof in his yellow Rolls Royce. He sent it off to Melbourne to have the work done. Later, when he wrapped the Rolls around a telegraph pole, it folded at the place where the cuts had been made. Rolls Royce, of course, wouldn't touch it to repair it and for years it was owned by the Perth Casino as a VIP courtesy car, its welded roof clearly visible through the surrounding yellow paintwork.

But that was in the late 1980s and, even though he was working nonstop, Wolf's approach to his lifestyle when he began his business in 1973 and for a long time afterwards was simple: "One thing I learned from the word go was that there was no money to spare for extravagance in lifestyle. That everything had to immediately be returned into the company. But having vintages from '66, '67, '68, '69, '70, '71 – that was the essence and I think the essence is the balance sheet."

With Wolf Blass reds doing so well, it was now time to introduce a riesling into the label. But where to find the grapes? W

A frugal family man

Wolf's aversion to debt has kept him afloat while all around him others have floundered as markets fall or interest rates soar. He abhors wastefulness, and even has a soft-drink vending machine in his office to keep track of such expenditure.

He instituted a signing-out process for his wine stocks right from the early days, one he participated in himself, even if he was giving wine to friends. And he likes to keep a close eye on household spending.

Yet he's a gambler and owner of racehorses, a hobby he estimates has cost him between $2 million and $6 million, depending on when you ask. He keeps a separate horseracing account to keep track of his wins and losses.

Soon after they were together, Shirley Nyberg-Blass wondered what on earth she had gotten herself into with this wealthy man – generous at times, almost miserly at others. When she moved in with him, he would put money in a tin and she had to keep a housekeeping book on what she spent from it. "You had to keep all your dockets and write down what you bought from the supermarket or wherever and keep the receipts and a tally in the book and balance it on a regular basis. It was the most odd thing I ever heard of and I actually had to do that for about the first 12 months of our relationship."

Even the contents of the piggy bank she had kept since she was a child was seized upon and banked.

"All my children and grandchildren, they've been allowed to go to that piggy bank if they want an ice-cream or they want something. The housekeeper needs something, she knows she can go to it."

Once, Shirley went away for a week and returned to find the piggy, normally sitting in full view and to the top with coins, strangely empty. Wolf had one of his staff bank its contents into his account. "I rescued it and now I keep it in a cupboard," Shirley says. After a year, Shirley closed the lid, so to speak, on the houshold petty-cash tin, but Wolf still keeps an eye on things.

Wolf also carries a change purse in each of his cars, where he saves

He did not indulge us. If we wanted something extra, we worked for it.

SHARYN BLASS

all his coins until there is a sufficient stack to have one of his staff bank them. "So he's very careful and cautious like this, but the next day he'll be on the phone putting a $10,000 bet on a racehorse; there's no balance," Shirley says. "But if he loses on a race he'll try and make it up somewhere else, so he'll try and buy some shares to balance it out. Or he'll stop having a bet for several weeks until he feels that he's game enough to get back into it again. He has total control over everything like that."

From the first time they met in London, Peter Perrin, Wolf Blass Export Manager from 1998, was given the message that expenses were to be kept to a minimum. Rather than a hotel, Wolf had an apartment booked for himself, Shirley and Peter to share. Recalls Shirley, "Peter was very nervous meeting Wolf for the first time and, of course, Wolf was an absolute bugger." Apart from insisting they take the Underground everywhere, Wolf instituted a thousand other tiny savings. "He went just a little bit too far," Shirley says, "and Peter said to me at one stage ,'I am sure this is a test for me, because he can't really be like this, can he, Shirley?'"

"Yes he is," she replied.

Bob May recalls an incident after the Foster's takeover. Wolf had plenty of money but not enough to do. He was looking for new ventures and a potential partner was entertaining him on the *Kookaburra Queen* paddle steamer on the Brisbane River. Wolf turned to Bob and said quietly, with considerable disapproval: "Look at this, Bob, they have Moet champagne, they don't need that. Look at them, they're just opening a new bottle and there's still half of another one. They don't need that. I don't like those things, it's just waste".

For Wolf, keeping an eye on the smaller details is essential to understanding and managing the bigger operations. He would always say to Bob May, "I want all of the financials all done properly. I want them there every month, I want them balancing." Despite their 30 years together, Wolf still expects Bob to explain what he is doing on his behalf.

"He likes the game, likes to very much do his own thing and be in control of it. One of the run-ins that I had with him was that, when we were running on the share market, I basically took control of a lot of the investing and just started doing it as I thought it needed to be done. I sold some shares because I thought that was the right time."

Wolf was on the phone the minute he realised, asking why Bob had done this without consulting him. Bob's response was because they had made a profit on the share sale and Wolf was away at the time.

"Well don't do that again," Wolf told him. "I don't mind you doing it, but it's my money, you talk to me about a decision of that nature."

"I just thought that was fair enough," Bob recalls. "It's not my money and I was starting to treat it as if it was. It was a fair cop; I'd gone over that border of client relationship and he had brought me back."

Bob sees Wolf as equally cautious with his children. "His kids have never had money thrown at them. Shirley and I might disagree on that but, for the wealth that he's got, he's been very frugal with them. He's

helped Anton out with the fishing business. He's helped Susan out with her husband and their business and he's helped Sharyn out, because he wants to have them working. Much of this has come from his upbringing. He'll say he had to do it for himself, out in the cold with no father or mother to support him."

Susan worked in hospitality before going to work for her father in what she described as "a made-up job" in the marketing department. He might have created a job for her, but he certainly didn't give her an easy ride because of it. He would chide her for leaving at 5.05pm when she finished at 5pm and she would say,

Wolf's daughter, Susan, with her husband Trevor and children, Braiden and Shae.

Wolf with his children, Sharyn and Anton.

Wolf's son Anton showing off his professional ability.

"Yeah, whatever, unless you're going to pay me overtime I'm out the door like every other person. I only have to work until five. I'm not like you and stay until seven."

Susan, who nearly everyone says is the most like Wolf of his three children, established and ran a successful spring water business with her husband, Trevor Gundlach, for three years without financial help from Wolf. Later they moved on to a motor-exhaust wholesaling business and, when a challenge came from an interstate company, they knew they had to get bigger or go under. This time Susan and Trevor accepted help. "Dad's helped us out in setting us up for a business and stuff like that and it's been great for us."

By the time Anton was born, when Wolf was 50, there was more wealth and the boy had a few more of the privileges that money could buy, although that was balanced by the pain and disruption of his parents' separation and the fact the Wolf was travelling endlessly. "I got exposed to a very privileged lifestyle compared to the girls. They would've had a nice lifestyle, but I got pampered and I got spoilt and got everything I wanted. All my necessities were taken care of if I wanted clothes or shoes," Anton says.

"Every time he went away on a business trip and I didn't go with him, he'd bring back souvenirs and toys and this and that. Not real expensive stuff, but he always made me feel special." Wolf helped Anton to get his Engineering Certificate and Skipper Grade 3 ticket for marine vessels. "The viability of the fishing industry is a concern to my father and the future depends on the sustainability of this industry. He's supported me 100 per cent all my life, but he doesn't spoil you like handing out cash to spend."

Sharyn Blass remembers how, as kids, when they lived part of their time with Wolf, she and her sister Susan were never allowed to sit around doing nothing. "It was, 'Off your arse, help me do this, come to the winery, do this. If you want your pocket money, then you better work for it.'

"So, from a financial point of view, he was never a giver. He did not indulge us, did not give us money for

the hell of it. If we wanted something, we worked for it. If we wanted something extra, as long as we worked, he was happy to help.

"At the time we thought he was a mean old bastard, but now we thank him that he actually instilled that work ethic in us. From my sister's point of view, and mine, we respected authority, we respected money, that's the way Dad brought us up. I think when Anton arrived he [Wolf] was just too old, he just didn't have the tolerance."

When she left school at 16, Sharyn worked for a year in her father's company as the office junior. "It was a fun time and I have to say I milked it. I just floated in, did a bit of banking, got away with blue murder and got paid. I knew I would only ever stay for 12 months. Working with Dad wasn't really an option for me."

Sharyn studied hopsitality in Austria, came home and worked in the industry and then decided to work as a volunteer in pet shelters. "Dad was just mortified. He was like, 'You're covered in animal shit and you're happy as Larry.' He didn't get it, that I was down there at the Welfare League with rubber boots on, masks

on, you know, cleaning out cages."

Wolf's reaction was no different to what many other parents might have said: "All the money I spent on your education and you end up picking up dog shit."

At the heart of Wolf's business succcess, and his frugality, is the example of the man who influenced him more than anyone else, his grandfather Otto Sohn.

In 2001, Wolf told Frank Heimans, in an interview for the Australian National Library, "I remember when I was very young my grandfather said, 'Never borrow money if you can't afford it.' The truth is, I have never run into financial difficulties. I said when I was a public company that if you start borrowing over a certain level that cannot be covered, I'm absolutely against this. I've never stepped over the mark on borrowing.

"When I was in rubber boots, a lot of my friends were very rich and I used to think, 'How the hell can I make money like them?'

"I could mention ten names like this who have all disappeared because they all borrowed money. They're all gone and I'm still here."

Wolf with brother
Peter, his wife
Patricia and son
Patrick, 1980.

Shirley and Wolf
with his brother
Fritz and his wife
Hanni in 2008.

Below: Annual reunion of old Wolf Blass Wines team. From left: Vic Patrick, Hugh Cuthbertson, Brian Walsh (guest), Wolf, Randolph Bowen, Paul Turnbull, Peter Perrin and John Glaetzer.

Above: Wolf with his staff, 2007. "There are a lot of people relying on me." From left: Meredith Cameron, Bob May, Shirley and Wolf, Judi Prosser, Elisabeth Ainslie and Marcia Richards.

Chapter 6

THE GREAT RIESLING ADVENTURE

Wolf with Jim Barry: "we started together independently and we helped each other" The 1998 Wolf Blass Rhine Riesling brought about some innovative marketing. "We were successful because we took the bull by the horns ... instead of going through a survey asking people and wasting our time."

In 1969, when he wanted to make a riesling, Wolf had trouble sourcing the grapes because Lindemans had 99 per cent of the available stocks under contract. Instead, working with his friend and fellow winemaker Jim Barry, he made a riesling blend with 30 per cent frontignac from the Clare and Barossa valleys.

Jim already had his own winery, vineyards and crushing and bottling facilities and a strong affiliation with the Clare Co-operative that gave him an inside running on sourcing grapes. Also that year, he made a 100 per cent riesling from the Barossa and Clare districts. The next year, Wolf made two 100 per cent rieslings, one from the Barossa and Eden valleys and another, which won his first medal for white, a silver in Brisbane, from the Clare Valley. "I didn't enter the earlier ones because they weren't good enough. When I won the silver I was over the moon because I didn't get good material."

But they were small bottlings. In 1973, in order to have a riesling in the range, he bought it already bottled from Jim Barry in Clare, as he still had no equipment to make his own. "I had to put a label on something." At this time, Wolf was known for his reds and white wine sales accounted for only 11 per cent of the domestic market. By 1981, 53 per cent of wine sold was white and Wolf was ready to roll with his contribution.

Although his initial effort, in 1978, was not an immediate success. When it was ready for bottling, Bob Cundy took it to Clare Valley with instructions

On holiday on the Gold Coast, Wolf's mate John Gordon tried to book a Saturday night table for eight, including Wolf, at what was then its most popular seafood restaurant, the Boatshed, on a site now occupied by the glitzy five-star Palazzo Versace. Then, it was a simple loft location with million-dollar views over the Broadwater. Not a chance, John Gordon was told. "Oh, well, I'm bringing Wolf Blass with me," he told the owner, who was on a quota of one carton a month of Wolf Blass riesling. "What about if I make that four boxes a month?" The entire dining room was rearranged to fit them in.

to add the sulphur when he had loaded it for transport (at that stage they were still moving products all over the Barossa on a couple of old utes.) But the winemaker misread the instructions and also added sulphur.

"It went kind of cloudy and Wolf didn't know what to do with it. But old Harry Brown, Wolf's agent in Sydney, came over and took the lot and the longer it stood the better it got," Bob says.

Wolf was uncertain whether or not to go ahead with more white wine. "I knew that there weren't any of a great standard in Australia, except for Orlando and Stanley and Leo Buring, and I was sitting there in a hopeless position of not having the grapes – nothing."

He kept on experimenting with whatever grapes he could get hold of, but it was only when he returned to Germany in 1978 to attend a

wine expo that he found the secret ingredient to commercial success. (Although Wolf reckons he didn't really produce a great riesling until the early 1990s, when Wendy Stucke was his chief winemaker. "Since then we've won bloody trophies and gold medals, but beforehand we were just ordinary.")

On the 1978 Germany trip, Wolf spoke about riesling at an international conference in Wiesbaden and visited wineries and former colleagues, asking what was new, and what could he do with the inferior grapes that were all he could get. It was only when he attended a tasting of Australian wines in Singapore on the return journey that inspiration struck.

After tasting so many different wines over a four-week period, particularly the rieslings in Germany and Austria, his palate had re-adjusted from the Australian products he had been tasting for so long. "I got a shock, because there was no flavour in the Australian wines. They were flat, they were, I would think, partially oxidised, they were not handled in a clean, crisp, fresh manner. They were stale, tired. Some of them were very good, but the average was not good. I said to myself, 'No, this can't be right. We can't drink this. We have to do something'. Although I wasn't really thinking about going in in a big way."

In Germany, Wolf saw that much had changed since he'd left, and winemakers were using grape-juice concentrate. He telephoned John Glaetzer from Singapore and told him to stop bottling. John's response was, "You must be drunk, Wolf" because they were just at the bottling stage. "I said, 'No, John, I am absolutely sober – do not bottle. Wait till I come home, we are going to do something with our riesling."

They did one run on their established system, called Bottling Number One, and another run that was super dry and put into oak, called Bottling Number Two. "This is so bad that you would sack someone for doing it. But we had Bottling Number Two in oak, not to really pick up the oak flavour, but to bring in a different style of dryness into that riesling. Absolutely dry, probably 2-3 grams of residual sugar. And then we did the adjustment of what I thought the Germans had done and we went in with 12 and 14 grams per litre sugar and looked at the CO_2 content."

Testing the market was straightforward, if a little unorthodox. The Bottling Number One, the dry wine made following their usual procedure, went to Western Australia. Bottling Number Two went to the eastern states. But they all had the same label. Then followed a massive national advertising blitz for the new Wolf Blass Rhine Riesling.

Not only was it very direct market testing, but it also set the gossip grapevine abuzz and gave the wine critics plenty to write about

because of the confusion it created. The West Australians were confused because it didn't taste new to them, which in fact it wasn't: as such, sales in the west were slow. But sales of Number Two "went berserk" in the eastern states. Once the last bottle of Number One was sold in the west, the company sent in the new riesling. It was, as Wolf says, madness. "Under any other circumstances and in any other company it would cost a marketing director the job. Anyway, we were successful because we took the bull by the horns trying to find out (in a big way) what can happen, instead of going through a survey asking people and wasting our time."

More remarkable, Wolf still had no access to top-class riesling grapes. "It was the blending techniques. We brought the best out of very ordinary material because nobody gave us the

Hyatt Hotel Canberra General Manager Karl-Werner Diefenbach (left) and the Chair of the National Hyatt Riesling Challenge, winemaker Ken Helm.

best – until later on, when we had our own grapes and we had the yeast propagation. That was when we really got stuck into it."

There were no awards for this amazing commercial success for the simple reason that it didn't have the finesse that you could only get from the best riesling grapes. "Riesling making is a very delicate thing. You have to have good

Gold Label Rhine Riesling

A premium but limited release, this wine has been specially selected for Qantas Airways world wide for first class passengers.

This wine is from the finest selection of our vintage each year, a classic South Australian wine from the world's most famous grape variety.

The wine will be available also from selected fine liquor stores, hotels and restaurants.

We are proud to be associated with Qantas.

grapes to start off with and this is an art in itself. Even today, we've probably only got 10 or 12 top-class riesling makers. They may all make riesling, but they are not bringing what you call the 'absolute top' out of it, because it is all something to do with the regulation of temperature, of crushing, how you handle your grapes, fermentation technique, yeast propagation, timing and everything else, under pressure or not, to get the best out of it.

"It is just a very delicate grape variety, which only the best winemaker can handle. But we had to make something good for the people to drink

out of the ordinary material which was available to us. It could have been some semillon, could have been some crouchen, we didn't ask, there were too many questions at the time. We worked on the palate, what is palatable, and I think that is where our strengths were, that our palate was superior to probably a lot of other people's at the time."

Long-time cellar manager Chris Hausler says: "It really took off because it was made to the consumer's requirements. It was a nice, sweet, easy-drinking riesling. In those days, there was a variety called Clare Riesling, which was crouchen. And you used colombard, that you used to get in from the riverland, that went in. And the grape juice was added to sweeten it. And then they had to get the gas levels right as well because it was slightly spritzig, which sort of gave it that freshness and that fruitiness."

The slight spritzig was Wolf's idea, to put in a little carbonic acid to lift the flavour. "I was just trying to make something more palatable and probably adding some artificial, imaginative thoughts behind the idea that somebody is opening a bottle and saying, 'Oh, yes, this is nice with some bubbles in!' Or something like that."

In fact, the Aussies liked it so much that Wolf soon had a problem keeping up with demand. "It was an unbelievable situation that suddenly Wolf Blass Wineries then became the No.1 seller in Australia after not making any white wine at all, because I was only concentrating on red wine

I think I was probably mad at the time.

WOLF BLASS

to start off with. And it became the most popular bloody wine in Australia. So if somebody wanted four cartons, I gave them two. Anyway, this was an incredible bloody performance and I think I was mad probably at the time, because when we started it was a very dry riesling semillon style, whatever was available, because I didn't have the best material."

In the face of sales outstripping their ability to produce, it was actually Wolf's accountant and friend Bob May who came up with the quota scheme. Bob began working for Wolf a half a day a week around 1978, when he was an accountant with McDonald Laing and Co. He was 30, conservative, didn't drink wine, only beer, and Wolf was his single biggest client. He had began working for him on a consultancy basis, which eventually stretched to the half-day a week arrangement and then finally to three days a week. At that point, Wolf offered Bob a 5 per cent share of the business.

"Being the conservative individual that I am,

I said no. That cost me a lot of money to do that, as it turned out. This was before the public company float. But I just felt at the time, and it's proved me right, that he and I would get on precisely because I didn't work for him, if I stayed independent. I can be fairly forthright and blunt at times and I've told Wolf a couple of times, 'Take your books and piss off. I've had a gut full of you.' But we make up and we move on. We're still skiing buddies."

Rather than being simply the company accountant, as the business went through spectacular growth Bob took on the roll of confidante and right-hand man. "It was my job to try and balance that growth and have the cash available." He also learned to deal with Wolf's practice of consulting everyone on every decision, from his winemaker to the cellar hand, his butcher and his baker. "And then he'd ask me and then he'd formulate his own view."

Wolf and great friend and business associate Murray Tyrrell celebrate Harry Brown's birthday. Harry encouraged Wolf to develop his riesling style.

The success of the Wolf Blass riesling in the early 1980s coincided with and contributed to problems associated with the company's spectacular growth in the 1970s. "The Wolf Blass Rhine Riesling ended up an absolute boomer and we couldn't supply enough of it." That in itself created enormous demand that could have actually sent the company broke if they'd tried to meet it. They couldn't get grapes, they would most likely start facing tax problems and, therefore, they decided to slow down sales at the same time they increased prices.

Bob suggested the quota system. If someone ordered 300 cases, they would get 100 or 150. That gave the company enough cash to fund growth in an organised manner, and that suited Wolf, who Bob knew was extremely conservative beneath his external flamboyance, although far from conventional – particularly in the way he established a selling price.

'Basically, he'd say, 'It cost me this much for grapes, it cost me this much for a barrel, it cost me this much for something else and then I'll add some interest on it.'" Bob would point out that Wolf's way of pricing did not follow standard accounting methods; for one thing, he didn't actually incur any interest. But Wolf just kept calculating the costs his way with a percentage for interest, a bit more for his retirement, a bit more for profit and then some more for risk taking. The grand total would be his selling price and he'd tell Bob, "I don't care about the conventional way, that's the way we are going to do it."

As Bob says, Wolf could do this because he was a marketing genius who told people: "Forget what the price is, you'll need to drink my wine, because my wine will do this for you."

But while Wolf's nature and marketing genius worked with a private company that was essentially a small, tightknit band with just one conductor – Wolf Blass—would it work as a public company? Bob May had his doubts. **W**

The Wolf Blass family tree

Platinum Label

Black Label

Grey Label

Gold Label

Yellow Label

Red Label

Eaglehawk

Chapter 7

SILENCING THE CRITICS

'We must win medals," Wolf announced early in his career in Australia. He then proceeded to carpet bomb the world with wines in the quest for them, mainly so he could decorate his labels, another successful marketing practice. These days, when consumers can sometimes barely read the wine description for the number of medals plastered over them from shows in unfamiliar places, it's hard to imagine this was considered a bizarre practice back in the 1960s. "I was criticised because I'd been to Budapest, I'd been to Yugoslavia, but the philosophy was quite clear to me. It doesn't matter where it is, as long as you win something – and you stick it on the label. And of course I was criticised for this. They said I couldn't win properly at home, but had to go to those 'mickey mouse' bloody international wine shows. But I always had believed the international wine was always one step ahead of the rest of the industry."

The first Australian awards for Wolf's reds went to other wineries he'd consulted for after he left Kaiser Stuhl. Woodley wines won gold, Bleasdale won medals and Basedow won the Jimmy Watson. "I never got the credit for that. But the industry took notice of me. There was no doubt about that, they knew I was something that was happening."

Wolf was devastated when, as a consultant, he was overlooked at the 1964 Royal Melbourne Show, having entered a category for the best wine in a vintage. "I threw everything in from these companies and I didn't get a bronze medal. That

" NINE OUT OF TEN IS PRETTY GOOD, WOLF "

Once again, Wolf Blass Wines has been judged Australia's most successful red wine exhibitor. And it's been that way for 9 out of the last 10 years. In fact, since our first vintage in 1966, Wolf Blass wines have captured an outstanding total of 2,575 National and International awards. Now that's a real Touch of Class.

was one of the most devastating days, I think, which I can remember in my life. Because I walked away not knowing what went wrong. Just thinking, 'This can't be right.' Because these wines had won prizes in other shows, I thought they were the best, but for some reason or another something went wrong. I just felt very, very down, because for the $2.50 an hour I earned I had to win some awards. I had to be a winner. And I just failed and I don't know why. I wouldn't have changed anything. It was an awakening."

Melbourne is the most highly regarded show in the country and, while he hated the failure, Wolf also wondered if his status as a newcomer and a consultant, the only one in the country and without a vineyard to his name, might also have come into consideration. "I don't think I was cocky to go there, but maybe they would say, 'His head is too big to get a hat on!'"

He had a sense of being an outsider, and says he resented that for five years the Royal Adelaide Wine Show insisted on inspecting his cellars to ensure he really did have commercial quantities of his award-winning wines. "For four or five years, they came and bloody checked up the bloody wines. They went to Basedow, they went to Woodley's, they had been a couple of times to Norman's, because Norman's won every year whilst I was there." Wolf threatened legal action against what he regarded as harassment.

" I think the old established wine families in the Barossa thought this brash, young German fellow was trying to go ahead too quickly, and because he was 'a blender' they thought he knew nothing about wines," John Gordon says.

The Australian awards in his own name began rolling in in 1967, when a Wolf Blass Limited Bottling Langhorne Creek Cabernet Shiraz won a silver medal at the Adelaide show. In 1968, it was the gold medal – his first in Australia. In 1969, there was silver and gold and, in 1970, came the first medal for one of his white wines – a Clare Valley Riesling. Eventually, there was such an embarrassment of medals that even Wolf could see it was too much. "This became suddenly also obsolete because we won so many medals, we hit the industry so hard, John Glaetzer and me, that it became obscene." It was time for a new philosophy. No bronze medals. "Bronze says it is just a fair-enough good wine."

From a consumer perspective, the Blass system of colour coding wines was a real stroke of genius, making selection incredibly easy. Wolf commissioned a local artist, Neil Tamke, and Wytt Moro, who had designed some wonderful labels for Woodley Wines. Cheekily, he used a shield given to him by his previous employer, Kaiser Stuhl, in recognition of his three years there. It read: "In remembrance of the service 1961-1964 South Australian Grape Growers Cooperative, Technical Section".

Then Wolf went a step further and decided to wrap the label right around the bottle. "Nobody ever believed such a label can ever be bloody successfully designed. I had to say something, 'Who I am or what I'm doing and this is why I designed this.'" He also added a grey label, keeping the yellow he had been using up until 1967, the first step in the wildly successful colour coding of his labels. "From the beginning, I had a very clear view on yellow, because yellow and chocolate brown, to me, were the most obvious colours for advertising. It hit me every time when I looked at this when we designed

things, and just as well I stuck with it. People would walk around the stores and they would say they wanted the Wolf Blass yellow label or the Wolf Blass grey label; they didn't go in there describing what grape variety they wanted, this wasn't important to them. The varieties were on the label, but I think the mastermind was that I made it as simple as possible for the consumer to identify the product, enjoy it, drink it and buy another bottle."

The colours were initially inspired by sports, because that is what most Australians know most about. Yellow Label was created after Wolf had watched a game of Australian Rules football with AFL legends Hawthorn, and he liked the yellow in their guernseys. After a trip to Asia, where the colour red holds great significance, Wolf launched the Red Label. Gold and Brown labels followed, then the Green Label, just for the Irish. Naturally, the first Jimmy Watson required a whole new colour of its own,

Award-winning winemakers. From left: David Wardlaw, Stephen John, Krista Binda, Chris Hatcher, John Glaetzer and Wolf Blass in 1990.

and the Black Label is still the company's most prestigious blended red wine. Platinum is the premium wine, a straight Barossa Shiraz.

There were some initial setbacks to those first wraparound labels, not least that no labelling machine could handle them. That's where an ever-present group of friends and family swung into action. Neil Tamke's wife Elza, John Glaetzer's future wife Margarete and Wolf's wife Raelene attached the labels by hand in the garage at their home in the Tolleys company house at Nuriootpa, from 1969 to 1973.

"When he was working for Tolleys, he was still doing I don't know how many tonnes for himself under his own label," Raelene say. "We were standing there with a hand glueing machine and I had Susan running around my feet. Oh, what a schmozzle."

The other big change Wolf introduced from the consumer's perspective was that he sold quality wines people could drink immediately, rather than having to lay them down for a few years to mature. "To me, it didn't make any sense. These wines were powerful, they had flavour and they were hand selected and blended by these respective wine companies I was working for. Once I won awards, of course, that got me up to six foot. This is when I started saying, 'I'm doing something.'"

As well as wine awards, Wolf started picking up packaging awards. He'd decided early on that, "if the presentation doesn't look right to the

buyers, they won't buy it." The corporate image developed at the outset may have changed in subtle ways over the years, but the label's overall image has never been altered substantially.

When they were first produced, with their giant eagle about to take flight from a nest of vine leaves and grapes, some called his labels kitsch. "But they are distinctive," was Wolf's reply. As far as he is concerned, they were and still are worthy of emulation. "We were probably the first to give precise information on the grape area and varieties used in a particular wine. We explained the blends of our wines on the labels and we got a lot of credit for that."

In 1979, Wolf answered his critics by staging the biggest wine-tasting Australia had ever seen. It was a huge gamble because his reputation was now publicly at the mercy of Australia's leading wine writers and judges. In Sydney, at Len Evans' restaurant at Circular Quay, 40 esteemed palates lined up to taste more than 35 Wolf Blass wines, mainly reds, made between 1966 and 1976. Wolf was uncharacteristically quiet. He admitted afterwards that the verdicts could have made or broken his reputation. He need not have worried. "The outcome could not have been better for him," Tony Baker writes in his 1991 book on Wolf.

James Halliday was among those at the tasting. It must have been hugely gratifying to Wolf that Halliday described the 1966 Yellow

The first Jimmy Watson required a colour
of its own, and the Black Label remains the
company's most prestigious blended red wine.

Wolf with Len Evans at the biggest wine tasting
Australia had seen, in 1979 at Circular Quay.
Evans told the cream of the country's wine
writers and critics, "If more people made red the
Blass way, the industry would sell a lot more red."

Label Shiraz Malbec as, "holding very well with an intriguing combination of big, old, rich fruit with some cool climate type characters". The 1967 Yellow Label Cabernet Shiraz was "outstanding"; the Yellow Label 1968 Cabernet Sauvignon and Shiraz was "outstanding with fruit still holding to perfection"; the 1972 Grey Label Cabernet Sauvignon and Shiraz was "fine and complex" and had "years in front of it".

Judge and critic Len Evans summed up the overall feeling. "If more people made red the Blass way, the industry would sell a lot more red." He noted that, although some people claimed Wolf's wines didn't last, the older examples still had plenty of life in them. At which stage Wolf interjected to point out that the only reason his wines didn't last was because they didn't have time to before people drank them all.

But Wolf was not about to rest on his laurels. The 1980s were to be another eventful decade, with the acquisition of a share in a bottling plant, a national marketing award and an international partnership with one of the great French wine and spirit companies, Remy.

He was also honoured as a Baron of the Barossa for his contribution to the wine industry, waged a high-profile and successful war against discounting, re-married, had a third child, divorced, met his future wife and achieved a hugely successful public listing. WB

Travelling with the man

Wolf Blass Global Wine Ambassador George Samios probably knows the man better than anyone in the company, having regularly travelled with him on promotional tours for the past decade. The pair run a practised line of banter behind the microphone, with George as the straight man.

Behind the scenes, it is George's role to keep his star calm (not always easy) and get him to the right place at the right time for the next gig. Once Wolf's on the way out the door, though, everyone has to step up their pace because he is so competitive. "Even if we are walking through the foyer of a hotel, Wolf needs to be in front," laughs George.

"Sometimes, I deliberately pick up the pace just so I can see the nostrils and eyebrows flare as he picks his pace up. He jokes about how slow some of his horses are … I reckon he could beat some of them. God help us if he was a jockey … if the horse was too slow he would probably piggyback it to the finish line."

After their double act at promotional

George Samios, Wolf Blass Global Wine Ambassador.

events, George then has to get Wolf back to his hotel, also not always easy. "I wish I had a dollar for every time a complete stranger comes up to Wolf and reminisces about the time they met him at the Wolf Blass cellar door 30 years ago." At the end of every event, there could be 50 people wanting Wolf to sign their bottle of wine and chat. It is George's job to call an end to the parade of fans to Wolf's table, or it would go on for hours.

Wolf is so passionately Australian, despite still speaking with endearing German resonances and sentence structures, that when he travels overseas he takes bags full of Australian souvenir badges and stuffed native toys to hand out to people he meets. "He always puts a stuffed kangaroo (often a boxing one) on the podium at every official event we host. At the end of the trip he saves the cutest stuffed toys for the local sales and marketing people who have hosted us. Funny, though … they never get given to males," George says.

Wolf also loves the sound of his own voice, and not always sticking completely to the subject at hand. Like the time he proposed the toast to the bride and groom at George's wedding. His ten-minute speech omitted any reference to the fine character of the newlyweds, instead concentrating on advice that a good sex life was the secret to surviving marriage, and that included good make-up sex after a fight. "To this day my friends ask me how is Australia's number one winemaker and marriage counsellor," George says.

Not that Wolf is above having a dig at those giving him an award. He told guests at the 10th Maurice O'Shea in 2000: "I have a short speech that I prepared in 1994, because that is when I thought I should have won this award." The speech lasted 30 minutes. At the end, a few wits decided he should also have an award for his prostitution of the English language.

George says: "Often I joke at the end of a Wolf speech that I have an English version on paper for those who did not understand what he had just said."

Wolf loves his sport, sponsors many sporting events and has a lifelong love of soccer. Wolf Blass are the official wines served at Old Trafford, the homeground of Manchester United. When Wolf and United's long-time manager, Sir Alex Ferguson, met it was a friendship forged in mutual interests. "Wolf wanted to talk about soccer, Sir Alex wanted to talk about wine, and they both wanted to talk about horseracing," George says.

People to this day still cannot quite believe that Wolf met the late Beatle George Harrison and had no idea he was a musician, even though they had talked constantly throughout a long dinner. "Such a nice man, he knows so much about soccer," Wolf pronounced afterwards, when people asked how he'd enjoyed the famous musician's company.

George Samios once asked Wolf why he continued to travel and promote his wine when he no longer owned the company. "If you had your name on more than 60 million bottles you, too, would do it."

Chapter 8

GOING PUBLIC

For any man, even one as driven as this, 1984 was just too big to handle. Wolf turned 50, his only son was born, he moved his home and his company headquarters from the Barossa to Adelaide, he went into an ultimately disastrous joint-venture distribution partnership with French Remy Martin, and he spearheaded a roadshow to launch the floating of Wolf Blass Wines on the Australian stockmarket.

The float was oversubscribed, a resounding success, but the price was too high for Wolf's second wife, Martine, their baby and the man himself, although he would only really face up to the emotional costs inflicted on all three of them some years later when his marriage finally collapsed.

His friend and chief adviser, Bob May, had been against going public. "I thought he was a private individual with a big public profile. He was larger than life and I didn't know how he would go on the big stage of a public company. My preference for him was to stay as he was and keep developing, because I felt he would struggle with the responsibilities to shareholders and dealing with the board, and he did in the early days. You can't have his flamboyance and openness with a public company."

But Wolf could see how fast his wealth was increasing and would ask himself, "What if it all falls over?" His rationale was that, by going public, he could avoid borrowing, to which he remained averse, and use the capital raised to fund more

The Eaglehawk goes public. Friends and employees were rewarded for their support. "I wanted our staff to take them. If they didn't have the money, I bloody loaned them the money."

growth. And the share value would be a clear indicator of what the business was worth if he decided to sell.

On March 13, 1984, Wolf Blass Wines was incorporated as a public company, acquiring Bilyara Vineyards for $15.2 million, with Wolf taking 60 per cent (18,839,994 50 cent ordinary shares) of a total offering of 31,399,994 shares. He had an option for an additional two million shares at a premium of 10 cents a share during the first half of the 1985 financial year.

In the preceding four years, Bilyara after-tax profits had increased from $.57 million in 1980-81 to $1.63 million in 1982-83. In the six months to that December, the net after-tax profit was $1.37 million. On the 1983-84 show circuit, Wolf Blass Wines won 72 awards for white wine, including 20 gold medals, and 79 for reds, 32 of them golds. From 1980 to 1984, he was Australia's most successful red-wine exhibitor. He'd had international successes since 1976 and, in 1981, the 1975 Black Label took gold at the Bristol International Wine Fair. There were growing export markets in New Zealand, Singapore, Hong Kong, Fiji, Malaysia, Macau and China.

It was a long way from the secondhand tin shed/piggery he had bought in 1969, and it had been a great ride to get here. But would Wolf the fun-loving winemaker, who liked nothing better than sporting events and drinking with his mates at the Greenock Business Luncheon Club, that famous long Friday lunch still going today, really be happy on a board? Yes. And no.

One of the first things Wolf did after deciding to go public was to ensure his friends were rewarded for their support over the years. Graham "Knocker" White, the National Australia Bank manager who gave him that first $2000 overdraft when he left Tolleys in 1973, Brian Linke, the Nuriootpa baker who loaned him money to buy grapes, and Peter Rosenberg, dear friend, horseracing buddy and one-time neighbour, were each allocated the maximum 30,000 shares. There was an allocation of shares to all employees – about 20 winemakers, laboratory technicians, cellar hands, vineyard hands and executives. "I wanted our staff to take them. If they didn't have the money, I bloody loaned them the money."

The float was handled by Goldsmith & Co in Adelaide as the primary underwriters, but the brokers were in for a few challenges on how it was to be handled. As Wolf puts it, there was a lot of "circus" about doing it his way.

"I offered shares to all our retailers, every retailer in Australia was approached by me personally in a letter form to take up shares, and Goldsmith didn't like this, they wanted to get to institutions, so there were a lot of arguments. My idea was to go to the people who were supporting me, to give them this opportunity, and they would want to buy more of my wines and sell my products. The shares had to go to the trade in order to entice them to be a loyal supporter to the Wolf Blass brand."

Wolf also released a special shareholders' label, a move he said was misunderstood by investors. "It was not really a great success. The shareholders thought I was going to con them or something." Nearly 30 years later, the few bottles left are still "bloody top class", according to Wolf.

Prospective investors were able to see a picture of steady growth and development from 1966 when the first Wolf Blass wines were produced in limited bottlings. In 1973, he began fulltime operations at the Bilyara Winery, which by 1984 covered nine hectares with an extensive complex of buildings, including a public relations centre, offices and administration and the capacity to mature 1,160,000 litres of wine in American, French and German oak, with stainless-steel storage for 3,200,000 litres of white wine.

Bilyara owned 50 per cent of the Australian Bottling Co (S.A.) Pty Ltd, Australia's first independent bottling company. In 1980, it had purchased and planted out a 49-hectare, undeveloped property in the Clare Valley, Sevenhill Vineyard, for its own use, despite Wolf's distaste for owning vineyards. But a grape shortage had left little option. "It was risk management, but Wolf was exactly right that it tied up a lot of money and caused us some difficulties post public company," Bob May says.

> *I wanted our staff to take them [the shares]. If they didn't have the money, I bloody loaned them the money.*
>
> WOLF BLASS

Says Wolf, "It was only when it really started getting bigger and bigger that we had to have vineyards, because I was in big trouble in 1989 and 1990, not only with the Remy Blass salesforce, but the grape shortage. That nearly killed the bloody goose, because I had to pay the high price, I had no buffer, because I had no vineyards, so that really shook the public company, temporarily.

"That is when I bought Tim Knappstein, that is when I went into Quelltaler, that is when I did Eden Valley, and then I started planting, put millions of dollars in so I would never get caught again. But by then I was marketing streets ahead, you know, I was marketing ahead, but the high price gave me a hard time for a short period."

Eventually, there was a supply spread of about a third from the company's own vineyards, a third from growers under contract and a third

Wolf Blass Wines board of directors (from left): John McDonald, Wolf Blass (executive chairman), Robert May and David Simmons. "Wolf had a lot of foresight to bring in directors from outside," Bob May says.

wine. As much capital as possible was kept for marketing and sponsorships. "To get the label on the market, instead of having the capital sitting in vineyards and in machinery," says Wolf.

In the run up to the public float, Wolf had asked Bob May to establish "my own little board" for Bilyara. It ended up as a closeknit management group with marketing manager Mike Fallon, winemaker John Glaetzer, lawyer Ian Edgley and Bob May, and it smoothed the way forward to becoming a public company. Ian Edgley went on to become chairman of Wolf Blass Wines Limited, Wolf became managing director and Bob May company secretary. "Wolf had a lot of foresight to bring in directors from outside. It's a thing that a lot of small businesses should do today, so that they don't get too insular," Bob May says.

By 1986, they decided the board needed to be extended to include some more establishment figures. Keith Smith, a former managing director of Wolf's first employer in Australia, Kaiser Stuhl Wines, the director of State Development in South Australia from 1984 to 1986 and the chief executive of Safcol Holdings, replaced Ian Edgley in 1986. In 1987, David Simmons, of the law firm Thomson Simmons & Co, was appointed to the board. "A three-man board was a bit lightweight with just an accountant with a local firm and a lawyer with a small law firm. We had to give the thing a bit more meat, just for substance with the investment community, and these

appointments gave us a bit more oomph," Bob May says. Initially, despite an awesome tally of national and international awards and a steadily improving balance sheet for an expanding business, the reception to the public offering was disappointing. The first letdown was that the establishment brokers, used to dealing with the "old Adelaide" set, were lukewarm about taking on the float, probably in part because of Wolf's reputation as a renegade.

Ian Edgley suggested Goldsmith & Co, where they found an eager young broker, Andrew Counsell, full of enthusiasm for the offer. His first suggestion was to go to institutional investors. Wolf told him: "No you won't, you'll go to the public, they're all going to drink my booze, I don't want these institutions and things in my shares." He gave Counsell a list of all his customers. "I want these people to own the shares, because they'll drink my booze." He genuinely wanted Joe Public to be shareholders.

But Joe Public was not much of a sharemarket investor back in 1983 and it took all Wolf's marketing skills to get him to the brokers. The offer laboured until Wolf decided to take a hand. "We're going on a roadshow, Bob," he said. This became common practice in later years, but at the time Bob's reaction was, "Wolf, you can't go out spruiking the share price." They did, of course, with Wolf bringing out the booze on every occasion, telling the stockbrokers, "I've got a bloody great company, it's fantastic. My booze is fantastic, we're going fantastically, so why do you bastards still only have the shares at 50 cents."

Ever the conservative, Bob sometimes tried to knobble Wolf's hard sell, without success. After the roadshow and the release of the first full year's consolidated net profit of more than $3.3 million, the shares went up to about $1. In 1986, the company bought 100 per cent of the Australian Bottling Co, which was upgraded to cater for still and sparkling wines and was being used as a bottling facility by more than 40 wineries.

The previous year, the company had acquired a 50 per cent interest in Remy Blass and Associates Limited, the joint-venture sales company, in order to boost international distribution. Given his instinctive dislike of the French, Wolf says he should have thought twice. "Remy Martin became a poison pill to our company," he says. And he had broken his golden rule – never enter into any arrangement where you don't have control.

"I had 49.9 per cent v 50.1 per cent, so that 0.2 per cent broke the camel's back, we didn't have any chance of rectifying a bad situation and therefore we were in big, big trouble, because there was no co-operation from Remy management." Unhappy with the French manager in Australia, Wolf was delighted to see him replaced by Kevin McLintock (who later became chief executive of McWilliam's).

According to Wolf, "Remy honestly believed, it was made quite clear, that they were doing too good for Wolf Blass, they should sell more bloody French products." McLintock was replaced by another Frenchman, Henry Terri, and problems escalated. "It could have been cultural – the French and German thing – but I never understood because they had a 50 per cent interest in making money. But nobody could ever work with the French, with the Remy Group, worldwide. Why should I have been an exception? It pushed us into a corner."

As part of the float, the company's headquarters had been moved to Adelaide. Although Wolf's marriage was already under strain as a result of his total focus on the business, and with Anton only four months old, he sent Martine to the city to set up a new home. Wolf was only home at weekends and Martine, a new mother, found herself with no close women friends to talk to about her concerns with Anton, in particular, who was a handful They both agree, in hindsight, that they should have stayed in the Valley.

Martine says, "Wolf needed support and assistance, despite the fact the marriage was starting to break down." When Anton was ten months old, Martine and Wolf left him in Adelaide with friends Yvonne and Fred Vella for three weeks so they could visit the Remy family in Cognac to secure and discuss the future of the

Icons of the Australian wine industry in 1986 including (seated from left to right) Peter Lehmann, George Fairbrother, Len Evans, Max Schubert and Jack Kilgour.

Getting the float off the ground and the share price

going was a great ego boost.

WOLF BLASS

Remy Blass distribution company. In 1986-87, in the face of a 2.6 per cent industry-wide drop in sales, the company's consolidated net profit rose to just under $3.5 million, up 5 per cent on sales that rose by 30 per cent. The company had 5.25 per cent market share on overall national sales of table wine and 18 per cent of premium wine sales. A share issue of 2.5 million shares had been approved for employees and executive directors. And Wolf was looking forward to the establishment of "the biggest and best" wine museum in the country, next door to the public relations centre.

In addition to achieving majority ownership of the prestigious white winemaker Tim Knappstein, in 1987 Wolf Blass Wines had acquired 90 hectares known as the Rogers Property in the Eden Valley. The company had also purchased the lovely 350-hectare Quelltaler Estate at Watervale, in the Clare Valley, with 137 hectares of vineyards and stone cellars dating back to the 1850s. It was renamed Eaglehawk Estate and the plan was to secure access to the premium white wine varieties chardonnay, semillon, Rhine riesling and sauvignon blanc. The purchase price was $5 million and the seller was Remy Martin. "We paid too much for it," Wolf says, adding another bone to his pile of contentions with the French. "We had to clean up the whole company, which was in a terrible bloody mess, and we had to invest a huge amount of money into the vineyard development, but I needed the grapes."

With Wolf Blass Yellow Label Rhine Resiling outselling all the rest, he had little choice, and even then had to buy wines from other regions, including the Renmark and Murray river areas and from Jim Barrie as well as Kaiser Stuhl.

"Fortunately, I could do this because I have a very good palate and I had good connections with people in these areas, so we could keep the bottling line going."

In 1987-88, net consolidated profit rose to just over $4.4 million; the following year it was up to $5.8 million. But 1989-90 was a tough year, with a 4.4 per cent overall drop in wine consumption, in part due to a strike by Australian airline pilots that hit the tourism and leisure industries hard. It was also a year of takeovers and restructures, with 90 per cent of the country's wine production and sales ending up in the hands of just 10 companies. Amazingly, despite the personal traumas of its executive chairman going through a painful separation and divorce, Wolf Blass Wines bucked the trend with not only an increased market share of 3 per cent, but a rise in consolidated net profit to $6.5 million.

But Wolf was beginning to sag. "Getting the float off the ground and the share price going was a great ego boost, but the actual operation of it all, the reality of what was involved, the demands of a public company and what they were expecting of a public company, it all hit in the next five years. He just had to get out," Bob May says.

According to Bob, fear of failure has always been a driving force within Wolf and the end of his second marriage, plus its effect on young Anton, were hard on him. "It was very hard on him. But he was still the same in his business. He wanted to know it all, know what was happening on the finance, know what was happening on the sales and know what was happening on the winemaking. Not because he was a control freak, but he just wanted to know, it was his responsibility."

Looking at the annual reports years later, Wolf says, "We weren't going bad, look at our sales, they were still up."

"And we weren't," Bob agrees, "because we were financially sound. But we had a couple of hiccups with the way that management had made some decisions and we were under scrutiny then, in the press and from the investors, because the share price was going down a bit. Wolf was having difficulties with his marriage breakup and he was going a bit wild then. As he says, he likes wine, women and song and he is a very carefree individual. But he had me belting him over the head, saying, 'You're the executive chairman of a public company, behave yourself.'"

A large part of Wolf's marketing spend went not on advertising but personally driven promotion, a sure-fire way to get publicity. Even if it wasn't always the sort that Bob May approved of, Wolf was untrammelled at the microphone. "I did black-tie dinners everywhere, with ladies invited, big functions," Wolf says. He was constantly appearing on popular lifestyle television shows, in the pages of glossy magazines and leading current affairs journals, in the financial press and the racing press. He was beamed across the world in a satellite auction of his wines run by Sotheby's.

He also spent on point-of-sale merchandising and displays to support independent liquor retailers under attack from discounting by large chains. "They were very happy with that because they made good profits because my prices went up and they knew that Blass wines are never discounted." Wolf refused to supply supermarkets who discounted. "I just didn't make deliveries to them." He even went to one supermarket in Brisbane and bought his wines that were on sale at a discount.

This kind of behaviour soon put him into conflict with national competition laws and Wolf was given a "please explain" notice from the federal government. "They said I was fighting discounting, but I explained my reason was that it was because I only had a limited supply." Wolf was given a stern warning. "That was very well advertised around Australia, my stand to make profit, and the small retailers loved me."

He also prepared and had published in the trade magazines a chart showing how much retailers stood to lose if they discounted even by 5-10 per cent. "I was telling them, 'If you idiots are going to discount the product (not just mine, but anything) this is what you lose in profit.'" Nevertheless, he retained good business relationships with the people he dealt with in the liquor divisions of supermarkets by putting money up for advertising of his wine, telling them: "It's not for you to bring the price down, it's for you to advertise."

He was still a comparatively small operator, so it was a risky time for him. "I was under the gun, alright, but I got away with it because I think the handshake meant something at the time. I shook hands with some great guys and they understood my policy."

But come 1989-90 and Wolf had had enough. "Two or three things [divorce, management problems in 1988 when he was travelling overseas extensively and the Remy Blass issues] were happening at the same time and then I was suddenly running the whole bloody show by myself. Which was alright, this didn't worry me, but what it did to me, it grinded so much away that suddenly for the first time I was thinking, 'I don't need all this! I think I better do something about it.'

"I lost a lot of faith in the people that I employed, because they had let me down. My kids weren't really interested in the whole thing, my marriage was broken up and I said, 'Look, the company has to grow bigger and the only way that we are going to do it is to be a merger.'" His directors were opposed to the move. "They said, 'Clear up your staffing and life will be much better.' But I thought to myself, 'Why should I? Why should I burn my energy? What for?'" **W**

AWARDS 1985

WINNER
**Small
Business
Award**
SPONSOR
**Australia
and
New Zealand
Banking
Group Ltd**

A strong personal and market presence and consistent high quality product mark the Blass success story. (Inset) Wolf Blass, managing director.

Taking the Wolf's share of the wine market

Wolf Blass has been described as the man who turned the prestige wine business into a kind of McDonald's affair on one hand, and as a genius on the other. Michael Kiely reports on a master wine maker who has a nose for wine and an instinct for marketing.

"I AM successful because I am not afraid to try things," Wolf Blass asserted recently in an interview with *Gourmet* magazine.

"I don't care if something has been done one way for decades. If that way isn't working anymore, I can change it."

Along the way from selling 10,000 cases per annum a decade ago to moving more than 300,000 annually today, Mr Blass has disturbed more than the dust on the Australian premium wine industry with his approach to marketing.

He standardised quality in an industry that thrives on circumlocutory discussions on the relative merits of vintages and regions. In a market where a new class of drinker was seeking guidance, he gave the non-expert average drinker something they wanted — a consistently good wine.

"When people buy wine, they want something they can rely on, a wine that doesn't change from year to year, a wine

they can order with confidence if they're taking the boss to lunch," he told *Gourmet*.

"Most people don't want to hear about good years and bad years; they just want to enjoy drinking wine."

The wine market swamped by the ubiquitous cask, bottle wines are doing it hard. Although the industry is enjoying record levels of consumption, 75% of it comes out of heavily subsidised cardboard boxes.

Profitable trading is also difficult due to oversupply which is fuelling fierce discounting at all levels.

Despite this, and new taxes, Wolf Blass has become a household name among Yuppies whose active lives don't afford them much time to study fine wines, just enough to drink them.

In the past four years, the Blass label has increased its share of the bottle wine market from 2% to 5%, reports marketing director Michael Fallon.

When Wolf Blass Wines International was floated as a public company last year, the float was oversubscribed by two million. The company was valued at $15.5 million, and already Mr Blass declares shares are selling 10 per cent above par value. The public obviously like more than just what's in the bottle.

Quality as strategy

"The quality of our product has been continually acknowledged in the wine shows," says Mr Fallon. "Medals are important in the Australian market."

In 1983/1984, three out of every four Wolf Blass wines entered in Australian wine shows won medals. He has won the Jimmy Watson Trophy three years in a row.

"You can hit and miss and do well in the short term, but when you've been consistently taking off medals and trophies for 10 years, people judge you as a consistent producer of premium wines," says Mr Fallon.

MARKETING WORLD

47

A lot was spent on personally driven promotion, a sure-fire way to get publicity. Wolf was forever on popular lifestyle television shows and in the pages of glossy magazines and news journals.

Above: Wolf with
Bernhard Ryf,
wine and spirit
delegates in Cuba
in 2005.

International
Winemaker of the
Year team 1998.
Back row: Chris
Hatcher, John
Glaetzer, Caroline
Dunn and Chris
Hausler. Front row:
Kirsten Glaetzer,
Wolf and Wendy
Stuckey.

Above: Wolf with
Max Schubert,
1986, the two
men who changed
Australian wine.

Wolf celebrates
his 70th birthday
with businessman
Michael Pratt.

Chapter 9

MILDARA AND FOSTER'S

South Australian Premier John Olsen with MP Ivan Venning and Wolf Blass at the opening of the new Wolf Blass winery complex in 2001.

Opposite: The Wolf Blass bottling and packaging facility opened in 2006.

Ray King, the chief executive at Mildara Wines, was known in the industry as the Silver Fox. At first glance, he seemed a strange choice of partner for Blass the Ebullient. Wolf had talked to John Spalvins at the Adelaide Steamship Company, then one of Australia's biggest conglomerates, which went into receivership in 1991, and to Hardys Wines. But after talking also to the international distillers Seagram's, eventually he sealed a deal with King over drinks at the Buffalo restaurant in Adelaide. After, they went home to Wolf's place and celebrated with tomatoes on toast.

"We talked to Spalvins, and he didn't take much notice of it. He undervalued the company by 50 per cent and then he wanted to make an exchange of shares. His shares were $7 and they finished up at 25 cents, so I would have ended up broke. Then Hardys came along and they were keen to put the two companies together, but then we were much stronger than Hardys. They were bigger but operated at cheaper price points, so I said no." Seagram's were interested in a partnership if Wolf would agree to be chief executive in Australia. "I said, 'Shit, I want to get out of this. I don't want to be any bigger!'

"That was when the two companies – Ray King from Mildara, Wolf Blass from Wolf Blass Wines – were both on tip-toes [but] there was no idea about merger or anything, we were only interested to find out what can we buy?"

Wolf had been travelling overseas almost constantly for a couple of years,

uncharacteristically taking his eye off the day-to-day running of Wolf Blass Wines back home. His marketing director, Mike Fallon ("a wonderful man"), set things up so he had a good group of efficient and trustworthy people around him. But, with Wolf away so much, eventually they began to wonder if perhaps they shouldn't be making the money for themselves instead of for him. Wolf recalls, "I had to clear some of the executives out with some payouts straight away and then I was sitting right on the top again. It was a very messy awakening for me."

With the company back on its feet, Wolf went overseas again, but there was more drama on the horizon, this time from outside Wolf Blass Wines. "Suddenly, I got the bloody message that Ross Wilson (chief executive of the South Australian Brewing Company) has bought Southcorp and its affiliated companies like Penfolds, Lindemans, Rosemount, etc, representing over 36 per cent of the total Australian wine industry.

"So I went 'bang' on the plane back home, knowing that we would have to grow, and which company can we get? Because he had bought them all. We had 5 per cent of the market share and he had 36 per cent. I said, 'There must be something. Can we get a small company?' It made sense." But Wilson was selling nothing. And this is when Ray King and Wolf Blass come together. They had 6.5 per cent of the market, I had five per

cent. So Ray was sitting in a similar position to me. Value-wise, both companies the same."

At the same time, the relationship with Remy Martin had gone from bad to worse. "You couldn't communicate … there was no friendship left, there was nothing there, and you didn't know what was happening on the other side. They are selling alright, but the marketing was not there, the promotional activities. Doing things right was gone and we had no control. My people, which I had put in to look after the salesforce, which is Remy, came home very frustrated. We would have had to reinforce things within our own salesforce, but then we would have to pay Remy out.

"So, anyway, suddenly it just happened that this Ray King situation came up." King had also gone to Ross Wilson seeking to buy a company out of the Southcorp acquisition; Wolf and Ray King met, one going in, one coming out of meetings at which they were told Southcorp had nothing for sale. The men talked and agreed in principle that they'd be better off together as a joint force with a larger share of the market.

Wolf's board warned he wouldn't get a good price, "because then brands didn't mean anything, they cost nothing. But I was pretty well determined and I knew that the company would benefit … the shareholders would benefit in the end. I was absolutely convinced."

Untypically, Wolf was prepared to accept that Ray King would be the boss. "We were two different personalities – there was only one boss and he made it quite clear that he was going to be the boss and I said, 'Yeah, you do the domestic and I'll do the overseas things and I will be quite happy with that.'" The two met in Wolf's penthouse in the Adelaide beachfront suburb of Glenelg to talk more. The next day, they took a walk together in their tracksuits, right into a gathering of industry colleagues going in to a board meeting of the Wine Federation of Australia. Their secret meeting was a secret no more.

Many predicted disaster with the combination of King and Blass sharing the reins, but Wolf realised he had to change, to step back. "I realised that you cannot fight if you want to be successful in this type of a big partnership."

The merger was hard on the small team of loyal people who felt very much a part of the whole Wolf Blass adventure. "I think Wolf had a sense of frustration and perhaps a little bit of worry about failing, in the sense that it used to be his and now he was selling it," says Heather Mitchell, brand manager at the time of the merger.

"When it happened, he was very sad for his people. He didn't want what happened to us to happen and it was horrible, just awful, and he said to me, 'Cookie, you're the best, you know I love you'. And I would never have left Wolf. The only way I would have left Wolf is exactly what happened. We got kicked out or one of us dropped dead. I was a loyal little puppy to the

end and I suppose I still am in a different way. He felt as though he let us down and I said to him, 'You've got to look after you.' The way things were going, it was the only thing that he could do." Blass staff stayed on for the handover to Mildara staff. "That was like wrenching my babies away and giving them to somebody else, which I hated doing, and then to see what happened, because it became just another brand to them," Heather says.

Some years later, at a function, Heather heard someone from Mildara say that the Wolf Blass brand was at the end of its life cycle. "I said, 'You are fucking kidding me aren't you? The Wolf Blass

The Silver Fox, Ray King, head of Mildara. He made it quite clear that he was going to be the boss. "Ray never really gave me a job. He knew I was important, but didn't foster me the way Foster's have."

The final Wolf Blass board before the Foster's takeover. Front row, left to right: Brian Healey, Ray King; second row, left to right: John McDonald, Wolf, Bob May, David Smith; third row, left to right: David Barnett, Peter Thomas, Richard Hazelgrove. Below, overseas directors, left to right: David Grant, Tadao Suzuki and Grant Gordon.

brand is at the end of its cycle? Are you people insane?' I'll never forget. I caught up with Wolfie and I said, 'What are they friggin' doing, this is out of control.' We had lots of good chats afterwards."

The merger was formalised in May 1991. The differences in the wines made by the two groups could be judged in part by the trophy and medal haul. In 1990-91, Mildara Group wines won 28 gold medals, 50 silver and 89 bronze. In the same year, Wolf Blass Group wines won 56 gold, 89 silver and 129 bronze at major Australian shows. In terms of sales, Mildara's most successful labels were Jamieson's Run and Yellowglen sparkling wine. In 1993, the Jamieson's Run label was used to spearhead the company's marketing growth and in the first full year of operation the trade press declared it Wine Brand of the Year. Its domestic sales increased 50 per cent, Eaglehawk increased 30 per cent. In what was looking like a self-fulfilling prophecy on the end of a brand's life, the Wolf Blass brand fell 1 per cent, from double-digit growth a year earlier.

The formation of Mildara Blass provided the opportunity to unwind the distribution with Remy and hand over sales of the Wolf Blass range to Mildara's existing salesforce. "We knew that the only way we were going to get rid of the French was with money, and in the negotiation with their representative – he was a solicitor from a big solicitor house in Melbourne and he was also a director of Remy Martin Australia – we had to pull out the $1 million cheque. They

Timetable for change

In 1988, Wolf realised that as a public company he had to become bigger to survive. He could see that the Australian wine industry was on the cusp of some of the biggest changes of its short life. By 1992, takeovers, mergers and acquisitions had radically changed the way it operated and the upheavals contined into the 2000.

- In 1989, Orlando sold a majority stake to international wine and spirit giant Pernod-Ricard and the merged company went on to acquire Wyndham Estates in 1990.
- In 1990, Penfolds acquired Lindemans from Phillip Morris, and South Australian Brewing then acquired Penfolds and renamed itself Southcorp.

- In 1991, Wolf Blass Wines merged with Mildara.
- In 1992, Berri Renmano acquired Thomas Hardy to form BRL Hardy.
- In 1996, Foster's, the big beer company, entered the wine industry for the first time in its almost 200-year history, acquiring Mildara Blass.
- In 2001, Mildara Blass was merged with Beringer Wine Estates of California to form Beringer Blass Wine Estates, the world's first truly global premium wine company.
- In 2005, Foster's acquired Southcorp, making it the world's premium wine business.

took the pencil and signed. Bang," Wolf says.

In the first full year of the new company, group wine sales rose 8 per cent on the combined sales of the two entities the year before. Domestic sales rose 6 per cent, compared with an industry growth of 3 per cent. But export sales increased only 17 per cent compared with an overall wine industry growth of 37 per cent, mainly because Australia was exporting at prices 12 per cent below the previous year, while Mildara Blass stuck to its policy of getting a fair return on investment. The UK market for Australian wines was booming, but prices were 26 per cent down on the previous year. As Ray King

told shareholders at the 1992 Annual General Meeting, the well-documented short-sightedness of industry pricing policies in the domestic market was being repeated in the export market at a time when rapidly increasing demand and a possible inability to fill that demand should actually have seen prices rising.

Wolf took on the role of deputy chair, meaning that once again he had the issue of attending board meetings, and these were much more demanding. "He is just not a person that likes to sit on a board. He probably says things that at times he shouldn't, because he is just straight out with it. And, really, you have to sit back and think about things first, if you want to be on a board, and that is just not Wolf's forte," Shirley Nyberg-Blass says. "He was forever putting his foot in his mouth and he would always come home to me and say, 'I have done it again, Cookie, I have made another faux pas.' Every time that he went to a board meeting he would come home totally drained, and he felt intimidated by Ray King, I don't know why. I dreaded every time he went to a meeting. He'd come home and he'd be totally stressed."

Wolf's issues with Ray surprised Shirley because, after their meeting at the Buffalo, she had been optimistic he was the right partner for her husband. When Wolf had said he didn't like dining out, Ray had replied that he felt the same, and he was the one who suggested instead having sliced tomatoes on toast back at the Blass apartment. "We sat in the kitchen and we drank some good wine and that's how we celebrated, and I remember thinking that this was going to work," Shirley recalls.

Ray was a more aggressive operator than her cautious and conservative husband, who was nervous about the company's ambitious acquisitions program. "But Ray had a plan, he knew what he was doing and he did get the share price up. So everybody was happy at the end of the day, but I think Wolf was often in conflict with him. They were different personalities and his way of thinking made Wolf a bit nervous."

Eventually, Wolf resigned from the board to concentrate on building the export market. "Ray King was a political animal and Wolf, in his normal, typical honesty, would come out and say it like it is and they'd jump on him. I'm not saying Wolf's not intelligent, but these were also intelligent people and they were dealing at a different level. Here was Wolf talking about the makeup of a cork and whether it's the right cork in the bottle or whatever and they didn't want to know about that ... that's an operational thing."

Wolf says, "Ray never really gave me a job. He knew I was important, but didn't foster me the way Foster's have. To characterise Ray – he was good at figures, excellent in persuading the board on takeovers, lifted the share price and revalued brands, but he totally underestimated the value of the brand Wolf Blass, and the marketing team lacked inspiration, foresight and innovation. A total frustration to myself. I resigned as Deputy Chair one month prior to the Foster's takeover, in order to be able to sell down shares and form the Wolf Blass Group of Companies."

Peter Perrin was export manager for Wolf Blass Wines and, after the merger, he could see the stark differences in the attitudes of Ray and Wolf: "There used to be a lot of to-ing and fro-ing between them. Ray is one of the great wine industry identities, how he bought all these different labels like Yarra Ridge and all these others, Balgownie, Rothbury, Saltram, and added them all into a portfolio. But he'd say brands have lifecycles and, of course, Wolf said, 'No they

A roving ambassador

Wolf has never been comfortable in a public company. "Shareholders and institutions, they want to see growth by volume and they want to see growth by income/value/return on funds employed, but miracles on both sides do not exist," he says. "There has to be the time of rationalisation and, in my experience, having been three times through the system of corporate structures, it is very hard to rationalise in a public company."

Always uncomfortable with borrowing, he thinks the ideal ratio is 60 per cent assets to 40 per cent borrowings. "All my life – I have never changed from this one. Once you are going to get over this you are going to be in the hands of the devil." There is also a risk in the wine industry of over valuing assets. "You can restructure your balance sheets, you can over-value either your vineyards, your pricing or your wine stock, but eventually it's going to bite you because you are only going to get a retail price on the reality."

Wolf travels overseas about 10 weeks a year promoting Wolf Blass brands. The company provides an allowance for his office and staff and expenses for promotional activities. "From the word go, I made it clear that I am Wolf Blass, I have got nothing to do with the corporate section. I don't work under contracts and I am not a consultant, either. They give me a budget, but I have got no financial interest as far as the company is concerned, except as a private shareholder."

His motivation, he says, is mostly emotional. "My interest is with the Wolf Blass wines, where I am constantly guest speaker, presenter, talking about the wine industry." As well as being an ambassador for Wolf Blass on behalf of Foster's, he is also a past President and a Life Member of the International Wine and Spirit Competition. "I think I am part of the icons of the wine world and I think this is the way I see myself.

"Without getting any high falutin' ideas, I think I may know more about the global wine industry than probably anybody else, because I am constantly on the move. And I can see things before they even happen and that's the way I have been motivated. I am emotionally attached to the company, otherwise, at my age, I would have thought, 'Look, I don't need this circus.' "

don't, think of Moet et Chandon and Johnny Walker Scotch.' But I think in his heart Ray knew he was on a winner with someone as passionate as Wolf driving the brand and the profitability in it." Peter enjoyed the showy Wolf of the 1980s, but the new corporate image of the 1990s was a different story. "I guess it was more sort of dignified with Ray King."

At the time of the merger, Wolf Blass shares were around $1.05 and the deal was on the basis of a 100 per cent share swap, plus $2 million for the Wolf Blass name. "But I should have kept

Wolf Blass Wines vineyards in the Barossa Valley.

the name rights for the wine only. Afterward I thought, 'Oh, shit, you are starting again.'"

In 1996, Foster's made a cash offer of $7.75 a share for Mildara Blass and, once Wolf accepted, the acquisition went ahead quickly, at a cost of $560 million for net assets, with the wine management fully retained by Mildara Blass. "Then came what always does happen in corporate sectors, that we had to become bigger," Wolf says. In 2000, Foster's bought California-based Beringer Wine Estates for $2.6 billion. "We realised there were huge management problems because initially it was a management buyout, which meant that most of the executives were fairly rich people or were very comfortable, and once you are going to have comfort in management the lean and meanness is not there in order to become really competitive." Beringer had several wine brands in the United States and Mildara Blass had 14 in Australian, but the Beringer Blass CEO was based in the US "There was a little rumble and tumble going backwards and forwards in Australia and we had domestic management changes which were inevitable," Wolf says. On the plus side, this American management offered a great boost to a plan hatched by Wolf and John Glaetzer to extend the company's public relations activities. They had asked Foster's Australia CEO Ted Kunkel for $250,000. Then Wolf visited California and saw the scope of the Beringer Cellar Door and Visitor Centre.

"I saw that they have got a $25-$30 million cellar door and visitor centre surrounded by great buildings and gardens and, well, I had to pull a tooth somewhere." The upshot was a $5 million budget for the Australian Wolf Blass Visitor Centre. More money was to come, with Foster's spending $30 million in 2001 to extend production facilities at Wolf Blass Winery, where at that point they still didn't even have a crushing facility. "This was the right decision, absolutely, in order to operate 80,000 tonnes of grapes in the winery. Foster's was actually running immediately with new management and built up the brand again to a very competitive, strong line and we were the No.1 by volume and by brand in 2003," Wolf says.

By the time the new Wolf Blass Visitor Centre opened in the Barossa Valley in 2004, Foster's had built up the Wolf Blass Wine brand to be the most successful in Australia. In 2005, Foster's acquired Australia's biggest wine corporation, Southcorp, for $3.2 billion. This gave it about 60 additional brands and made it the world's leading premium wine company. By 2009, it was selling 500 million bottles of wine a year, with major markets in the United States, Australia, the UK, Canada, Ireland, Asia and Scandinavia.

It had a third of Australia's domestic bottled wine market. In 2006, Foster's completed a $75 million bottling and packaging facility at Wolf Blass Winery, able to produce 24,000 bottles an hour. Seventy per cent of the 65 million bottles produced there for export are from Wolf Blass.

In early 2009, Foster's CEO Ian Johnston, in response to customer demand, announced a renewed focus on its wine business by simplifying its portfolio and creating a more specialist wine salesforce. Wine would no longer be marketed under a "multi-beverage" model together with beer, cider and spirits. The move delighted Wolf, not least because he felt it was in the best interests not only of the iconic labels such as Penfolds, Blass, Lindemans and Saltrams, but also for the Australian wine industry generally.

Wolf had long been a critic of the concept of a one-size-fits-all salesforce for wine and beer. He believed a beer or spirit salesperson simply did not have the specialist knowledge of wine or the winemaking industry to sell a product so reliant on perception and promotion. "I think the management of Foster's decided that because of its so-called strengths in the beverage industry they could probably dictate terms." But it failed.

The global wine world was now prepared for a more dynamic approach, concentrating on the top, quality-end of the wine production. "There was to be a second salesforce put in place, which is what we had with Mildara Blass." WB

Chapter 10

BLASS CONQUERS THE WORLD

In 1980, Wolf Blass Wines sent its first export shipment to Singapore, to the Wine and Food Society there. It was the beginning of a major push into the global market that would see the company expand within the next decade to the US, Canada, the UK, Asia and Oceania and the Pacific. It also saw the first contact between Wolf and the French company Remy, through the Singapore agents Remy Nicolas, who became that country's official agent for Blass. It was such a successful partnership on a personal level with Remy Nicolas marketing executive Koh Chin Lian that the yellow, grey and classic dry-white labels became the country's most popular wines. Wolf spent a lot of time there, talking to sommeliers, and Singapore Airlines used him to train their staff.

In 1983, Wolf launched a big promotion in New Zealand, the country whose wine industry he had dismissed as "hillbilly" back in 1964 when he briefly considered accepting a job there. "We just went from one microphone to the other. It was just an absolute Blitzkrieg. We were in the press, doing television interviews, radio, media, we had great functions, black-tie dinners, including women, in Auckland, Wellington, Christchurch. We hit everything but the kitchen sink and that was just an exciting and a dynamic approach to getting Wolf Blass totally launched in all directions in the New Zealand market," Wolf recalls.

The New Zealand industry was still very small, trying unsuccessfully to make red wines, but defeated by climatic conditions. The country's thirst for red wine could

Top: Wolf Blass, with outgoing president Paul Symington, is appointed President of the International Wine and Spirit Competition in November 2004.

Bottom: Wolf with wife Shirley Nyberg-Blass in the Guild Hall of the City of London.

only be slaked by imports and Wolf Blass was at the forefront with the 1979 Black Label Cabernet Sauvignon and 1980 Yellow Label Cabernet Sauvignon Shiraz, along with the Wolf Blass 1982 Rhine Riesling and a Wolf Blass 1991 Classic Dry White. Marlborough, later the benchmark region for New Zealand white wine, was just getting established, and Wolf was one of the first Australians to see its potential.

In 1989-90, his company established a joint venture, Marlborough Cellars, with Corbans Wines, investing $4 million, which included building a $1.3 million production system to produce sauvignon blanc. Blass viticulturists did the blending of the local product with Australian grapes. "I believed that it was imperative for an Australian leading wine company to participate in what I classified the best sauvignon blanc in the world," Wolf says. "I thought, without sauvignon blanc from New Zealand, we would never reach great heights. And that has been proven by time."

Familiar labels in Australia were given a lift with the addition of the New Zealand wines, Eaglehawk Fume Blanc getting a 20 per cent infusion of Marlborough sauvignon blanc and the Chardonnay Cuvee enhanced by New Zealand pinot. In 1991, the company produced a 100 per cent Graystone Wolf Blass Cabernet Sauvignon from New Zealand under a newly designed label. "It was magnificent," Wolf says.

But the New Zealand interest was sold by Mildara Blass for $7.6 million in June 1993. "I

pleaded with Ray King not to get out of it, but he thought it was too hard to handle." Five years later, Foster's bought the complex for around triple that price.

Initially, the deal with Remy and Associates produced good results in terms of opening up markets through Remy International in Europe, Denmark, France, Singapore and Hong Kong, including a first shipment ever to Paris, to 400 Nicolas Wine Stores. The management and sales team of 80 was headed by Kevin McLintock, but when he resigned, Wolf believes, a conflict of interest developed between the wine and spirit divisions and by 1990 this had impacted on Blass wine sales.

In 1987, Wolf Blass Wines International signed a distribution agreement with Sainsbury in Vancouver for exclusive distribution in Canada. It was the era of the wildly successful Paul Hogan "shrimp on the barbie" Australian tourism promotion and, at a function for 500 people, a cheeky Aussie with a German accent was able to get away with some less than diplomatic remarks to the chairman of the Canadian Liquor Control Board.

"I asked him why he didn't allow Australian wines over $7 to enter Canada and in my funny, probably humorous, unscrupulous way, I told him that I would go home and tell the Australian wine industry that there should be no good quality wines being sent to Canada, because they don't understand and don't give their consumers the opportunity to see what we can produce. You could hear a needle dropping in that place. I think the Australian industry people thought this was the end of us." But, later that night, at the commissioner's invitation, the two met for a drink – a whisky – shook hands and within two weeks the first Wolf Blass Grey Label (priced at $15) left Australia for Canada for sale in independent cellars.

Wolf Blass Wines International newly appointed export manager Peter Perrin was at the dinner and recalls being horrified by Wolf's audacious speech. "I remember thinking, 'Oh, well, I don't need to come to Canada anymore.'" Later, he realised that Wolf's message was, "Don't benchmark Australia at a price point. With Australian wines, if you pay $10 for a bottle you'll get a good one, if you pay $15 you'll get a better one, if you pay $25 you'll get an even better one. Wolf's argument was that doesn't happen with the French. They've got to make the wine the same year from the same place, year in, year out, and they say it's good every year, and it isn't. Whereas Australia, it's got that ability. He was just making that point."

Also in Canada, Wolf attended a charity auction and was top bidder, at $6000, for two bottles from the great French chateau houses. "These were the type of wines you usually buy and just leave there and walk around and tell your mates you have got a bottle. While I was at the microphone, I asked the people from Chateau Latour for a corkscrew

Ein Berner war der Schnellste im «Château»

Bernhard Ryf (rechts) demonstrierte unbernische Schnelligkeit: Der Weinhändler vom bekannten «Wyhus Ryf» in Muri lud nämlich zum allerersten Club-Abend im neueröffneten «Château Mosimann». Der Meister Anton Mosimann (2.v.r.) zelebrierte das Menue höchstpersönlich, war doch der Ehrengast von Ryf auch ein Meister seines Fachs: die australische Weinlegende Wolf Blass (links), der höchstausgezeichnete Winzer gab sich mit seiner Ehefrau Shirley die Ehre

straight away and I opened the two bottles with all the wine industry around. I had publicity everywhere because they said, 'This bloke is bloody mad.' But I made quite sure they knew that Blass was the man who bought the wine."

When in 1987 Wolf signed a national distribution contract with Buckingham Wile, a division of the biggest single American distributor, Whitbread, he thought the US was won. "We

Wolf and Shirley in Canada, where he made top bid for two bottles of French wine and opened them on the spot. "I had publicity everywhere because they said, 'This bloke is bloody mad'."

Wolf Blass with Chris Hatcher and John Glaetzer after being named International Winemaker of the Year in 1988.

Wolf Blass capitalised on the famous "shrimp on the barbie" campaign promoting Australian products overseas. Below: With singer Olivia Newton-John and actor Hugh Jackman at Australia Week in Los Angeles.

thought, you know, 'We are on the moon. This is going to be a big, big start for the company.'" The partnership with Buckingham Wile came about because he was German. "Some German executive in this company saw me acting in some of the promotional activities which I did around the world. So he talked to me, and I remember this very clearly, he said, 'Why can't we do something together?' And this is how it has happened."

Contracts were signed and the Wolf Blass one-man travelling sales show went on the road across 35 states of America. With different liquor laws in every state, it was a tough gig. "It was a nightmare because it wasn't a matter of asking how much people could sell, but whether they would even accept the brand. But we became known and with the first shipment we put a small pamphlet on each bottle, all this had to be done by hand, to identify ourselves." The German background probably broke through a general ignorance about Australia's ability to produce a premium wine. "I think it was a matter of, 'Oh, he is a German winemaker, he must be alright.'" With Blass premium reds and whites in US warehouses and in the hands of a distributor established in 1742 and still going strong, the way ahead was looking good.

"Then came a big shock. There was a takeover by an international corporation, and in any takeover, even a friendly one, you are going to find morale goes down and the sales go down with it. There was no further investment made in purchasing wine or anything like this. So we fell off

the horse." Lindemans was already stronger in the American market, although with a cheaper wine, and when the new company released Wolf Blass International from its Buckingham Wile contract it moved, in 1990, to Seagram's, which would represent them in the United States and the United Kingdom. "But they didn't take us really seriously in America and I thought, 'Here we go again, we are going to have the same problem constantly – America, America, America.'"

The problem for Blass in America this time was that the Seagram Chateau and Estates Wine Company there represented the leading French chateaux with big names like Petrus, Latour and Mouton-Rothschild. "So we were just a straw in the ocean." As well, European and Chilean wines were starting to compete at the cheaper end of the market.

Wolf had been watching the progress of Australia's most successful exporter to America, Lindemans, also at the cheaper end of the market. In 1988, Peter Perrin, who had launched Lindemans in the US, was keen to return to Adelaide and joined Wolf Blass International as export director. "He knew already the tricks. He knew all the states, he knew all the ins and outs," Wolf says. In 1991, Mildara Blass bought American distribution company Benchmark Wines from Orlando, which was marketing Orlando and the Black Opal brand in the US. "They had the connections, they had people there, they had an

Robert Mondavi, Chairman of the Mondavi Corporation, presents Wolf with The Robert Mondavi Trophy at the Guild Hall in London in 1992. Chris Hancock, President of the 23rd International Wine and Spirit Competition, looks on.

office there and everything else. Instead of having Black Opal and Orlando wines, they did Wolf Blass and Black Opal. We probably paid too much for it, but at least we thought this was going to be a start for us to get in. Now we had a foot in the door and Peter was doing his job in America."

But there were still some problems in the United Kingdom. After Seagram's, the new distribution company, Hedges and Butler, was taken over by Denton Royce, which wanted volume sales through supermarket chains such as Tesco and Sainsbury's, while Wolf insisted on retaining pricing control and positioning as a premium brand. "We ended up setting our own operation up in the UK. I moved a guy from New Zealand first and then a local guy over there to run it. In the end we had our own import company in the US, the UK and in Asia, which we established in Singapore," Peter Perrin says. This happened at about the same time as the Mildara merger, which provided a bit more capital for investment in the export market.

In 1992, Wolf Blass won the international wine industry's most prestigious award, the Robert Mondavi Trophy, as International Winemaker of the Year, at the International Wine and Spirit Competition in London. It was the only Australian winery among the 10 finalists, which came from France, Italy, Germany, the US, New Zealand and South Africa.

By now the company had markets in 30 countries and Wolf Blass wines had been enjoyed by travellers on seven different leading international airlines and several shipping lines, including the grand dame of them all, Cunard, with its famous *Queen* liners. Exports had risen in value from just $354,386 in 1984-85 to $4.6 million in 1990. In 1991, the newly formed Mildara Blass was holding its nerve and determined to continue to concentrate on premium wine exports, despite the explosive success that year of other Australian wine companies selling cheaper products. The same policy has been followed by Foster's as the company continues to use its greatest living asset, Wolf himself, to travel the world as wine ambassador for his brand.

"The first time I saw Wolf in person was in New York at an Australian wine tasting and, 'lo and behold, there he is standing behind the Wolf Blass stand pouring his wine. It stunned me," Peter Perrin recalls. "It was a big, successful company and there he is sitting and doing that." Assuming this was just a one-off, Peter was more amazed to see Wolf back the next day at the stand, still pouring wine.

"He was there every hour of every day, standing behind his Wolf Blass stand and, of course, all the Americans are coming along, they didn't know who he was, they thought, you know, who's this funny little guy with an amazing accent, but an incredible personality, which the American's took to as well. My stand was two away from him and I'll never forget it; I'd be there pouring wine and the crowd would just get bigger and bigger around Wolf and he'd be laughing and pouring and just loving it. It was just amazing that he'd put all that effort into it while all the other companies only had the export managers like me there."

Peter believes the fun factor contributed to the early success of many Australian wines overseas, and Wolf Blass in particular. "You'd always have a bit of fun, and in a lot of ways I guess that was what was successful for Brand Australia in a lot of those tastings we did in America and everywhere. At the end of the day there'd be the Penfolds guy, the Rosemount guy, there'd be Wolf, there'd be Bruce Tyrrell, and they'd all be in the bar afterwards having a drink, talking about it together. You would never see the French or the German's doing that at any of these dinners. They'd go off home and they'd go to bed. The Aussies were always doing something, and Wolf just took that and kept it going."

This fun factor worked so well in Ireland that Wolf Blass became the number-one label, helped along by the fact that the distributor for many years was Dillon and Co, an established company that didn't get taken over or go broke like so many others had. "They loved Wolf, they loved the brand, they got behind it, they would bring in full containers. And they understood the philosophy of the pricing, that it was a premium-priced product. It was a flavour profile. They showed people what the wine was all about and that it was worth the price. The Irish got it."

In Ireland, Wolf particularly liked the fact that even people in opposition in business would get together. "You'd get the different retailers and hoteliers together, make a big presentation, and by about 11 o'clock they were not bloody looking at each other as opposition. They were all bloody getting into dancing, having a real party. So it was very easy, if you had the right mentality, to join the bloody fun, to get the guys behind you."

Peter Perrin came up with the idea of producing a Green Label Shiraz just for the Irish market. That went over well, so they brought out a 125ml bottle because, essentially, the Irish were not big wine drinkers. Then came the half bottles of Yellow Label Shiraz and Chardonnay, successfully promoted as a chance for two people to buy a bottle of wine to share.

Soon after joining the company, Perrin proved himself as more than just an American market know-how kinda guy when he signed a distribution deal with Sansho Shoji Co Ltd and the first shipment of Wolf Blass wines was sent to Japan, in 1990. "I think New Zealand and Asia were the first export markets because they were the easiest," Peter says. In those days, the domestic label could go straight into those markets and there was also the relationship with Wolf Blass and the Remy Martin company themselves, because Cognac's huge and you can sell it anywhere in South-East Asia. That gave us a bit of an in because Remy had their own operations in Singapore and Hong Kong. I think Asia and New Zealand, being close, also got the feed off the Wolf Blass phenomenon in Australia being high quality, no discounting, we don't cut on anything, a lot of oak, the distinctive style of the Wolf Blass product."

In the early days, expatriates were the main wine buyers in Hong Kong and Singapore and, because of the buzz about the label back home, they were demanding Wolf Blass. "They just didn't want to drink Nottage Hill and Jacob's Creek. They wanted the top Wolf Blass, they wanted Black Label and they wanted the premium," Peter says. The demand led to the establishment of Wolf Blass Asia and later Mildara Blass Asia in Singapore. Sales were also boosted by the appointment to the board in 1990 of Tadao Suzuki, president of Japan's biggest wine and spirit company, Mercian Corporation, with holdings in France and the US.

"The important issue, which we must never forget, is we were always people-orientated," Wolf says. "We always had people from the hotels, directors, food and beverage directors, every bloody where we went, we had a good roll up of people attending dinners or lunches. And, of course, the wine writers and critics at the same time. They all turned up every time when we did functions."

Peter Perrin believes the Asian market will never have the potential of North America while it remains mainly expats, but that it is changing as international tourism operators push for a reduction in import duties running as high as 400 per cent. In 2009, Asia sales were growing considerably and duty-free sales were a very big part of the market. "It's growing every year, but it's still a very small market in world terms. I don't think the culture is there yet for wine consumption," says Wolf, who enjoys visiting Korea, "because they have more fun than the Japanese. To promote you have to have a sense of humour and fun. But the Japanese are more reserved."

Wolf discovered this when he once slipped into a limousine beside a Japanese executive and, in his usual style, attempted to break the ice with a joke. "The Japanese and the Germans have a lot in common," he said, "we both came second in bloody World War II." As a joke it was as flat as last night's opened Champagne. But, despite this early apparent cultural faux pas, Wolf is confident about Japan. "If we maintain the same quality standard and have this continuous drive of not making any mistakes, keeping our eye on the global side, we will be as successful as we have been in Singapore [No.1], Canada [No.1], Ireland [No.1], Switzerland [No.1], England [No.3] and America [No.5]. And I think it is also going to happen that we are going to have Japan in a very strong

Left to Right: David Simmons (Wolf Blass Board Member), Yasujiro Iwasaki (President, Sansho Shoji), Wolf Blass, Bob May (Wolf Blass Board Member), Hirokazu Kasai (President, E.I.E. Enterprises Inc.), Greg Brigden (General Manager), Wolf Blass, John McDonald (Wolf Blass Board Member).

JAPAN-LAND OF THE RISING SALES

The maxim "Success Breeds Success" certainly applies to Wolf Blass Wines.

As a result of its domination of the Queensland market, Wolf Blass Wines has experienced a demand for its product in the affluent and very brand-conscious market of Japan. Explaining the connection, Wolf Blass Export Manager, Mr Peter Perrin, said Queensland was a favoured destination for Japanese honeymooners and holiday makers.

"Because of our huge presence in Queensland, many of these visitors see and taste our wines", Mr Perrin said.

"The result is an increased awareness and appreciation of Australian wine, which naturally they take with them when they go home," he said.

To capitalise on the trend, Wolf Blass Wines has signed a $150,000 export contract with one of Japan's leading companies, the Sansho Shoji Corporation.

The contract means that Wolf Blass Wines will soon be on the shelves of three major Tokyo department stores — Mitsukoshi, Hankyu and Seibu — and negotiations are continuing with six other stores throughout Japan.

"The move sits very well with our marketing philosophy of exporting Wolf Blass wines to the World," Mr Perrin said. "We are not just in the business of selling wine, but promoting brand awareness. And we are about to do it in probably the most brand-conscious market in the world".

Three red wines, the Black Label, Brown Label and Red Label along with the Classic Dry White, Rhine Riesling and the White Label Semillon have been earmarked for the Japanese market.

The first part of the shipment left for Tokyo in January, with the second scheduled for departure in August.

"Naturally we are aiming for the top end of the market," Mr Perrin said.

Wolf Blass Wines now exports to more than 30 countries, with export sales during 1990 expected to exceed $5.5 million.

Peter Perrin, Wolf Blass Wines Export Manager & Koh Chin Liang, Senior Marketing Executive, Remy Nicolas, Singapore.

SINGAPORE FLING!

A formal wine tasting dinner was held at the New Orleans Restaurant, Holiday Inn Parkview, Singapore recently to launch the new vintages of Wolf Blass Wines. Over 100 guests gathered to sample a beautifully prepared creole dinner cuisine matched to the Wolf Blass Wines.

Export Manager, Mr. Peter Perrin spoke on the success that Wolf Blass Wines were enjoying in the ever-growing Singapore market, and added that Wolf Blass was the only Australian producer that has wines now available at the world famous Duty Free Changi Airport.

Pictured is Mr. Peter Perrin with Mr. Koh Chin Liang, Senior Marketing Executive of Remy Nicolas, Singapore, before welcoming guests and being watched over by the boss!

Soon after joining the company, Peter Perrin signed a distribution deal with Sansho Shoji Co Ltd and the first shipment of Wolf Blass wines was sent to Japan, in 1990.

situation: South-East Asia is going to come in and China will follow the trend.

"China is not a priority for us. Our priority is America and South-East Asia, where we have started. You cannot be everywhere. You have to take it step by step in order to succeed. You will never succeed making a fast buck in a fast move anywhere and spending millions of dollars in advertising. So therefore China is a very long-range project, which could be 10, 15 years. So therefore I think we will be carrying on in the tradition of what we have been doing for 50 years – quality, character, consistency."

As Wolf points out, he has tackled tough markets before, places where the first step was to tell people that Australia actually makes wine. "I knew that Australia wasn't big enough if you wanted to grow – when I got here it was nine or 10 million people [now 21 million] – and that you had to go overseas in order to get recognised. But it was a very hard road to start off with because you had to explain that Australia is actually making wine, not just what type of wine is Australia making."

Peter Perrin agrees. "It was pretty darn hard to get that across into North America and into Europe, especially North America to start with, because you'd go over there and they'd look at it and say, 'This is an Australian wine? It's got a big eagle on it, it looks a bit like a can of Budweiser and it's called Wolf Blass?' So it was almost a barrier there, and the same in the UK."

Since changing the name was obviously out of the question, the company stuck with those first principles of making and marketing "quality, character and consistency", the philosophical message decided on by Wolf and his mates way back in the 1960s on that fishing trip, and which still underpins everything. "Because it did have that character about it, and because it was a quirky name, and an unusual name for an Australian wine, it was easy for people to remember," Peter says.

With his marriage over and Mildara Blass up and running, Wolf was eager to keep travelling overseas building exports, happy to leave the day-to-day management to Ray King. "For me, using him [Wolf] as the ambassador for the brand was a great bonus," Peter says. "People would say, 'Hey, the guy whose name's on the label is actually here and is keen to do promotions and has a personality you can't jump over.' He would just draw a crowd. He's a likeable, passionate man about what he does, and so that side of things was great.

"But there was still the economics of the business, that it was always more expensive than our mainstream competitors like Lindemans and Jacob's Creek, and people in the US market would ask how come we were from the Barossa, too, but we cost more? America was the big push because Lindemans had broken through; Australia was the flavour of the month. Instead of having Australian wines on the shelf next to the sake or the kosher wines, there was actually a bit of interest in Brand Australia."

Just as in the UK, there was huge pressure to reduce prices so agents could fill their containers and distributors could get the product into the mass market. "There was always an issue of having that three-tier system with us, the producer going to a distributor or an importer, then them selling it to a wholesaler. Whereas here in Australia we had our own operation, which was Wolf Blass or Remy Blass, and you would sell straight to the retailers. And at that stage a number of our competitors, specifically Lindemans and Jacob's Creek, were setting up their own import companies, and we were even further behind the eight ball."

Ray King had not been much interested in export with Mildara, and still wasn't particularly. Fortuitously, however, he had virtually inherited an export business when he bought the Black Opal brand, which had become something of a phenomenon in the US. More importantly, from Peter's perspective, it had an import licence established by a marketing consultant called Ray Cashmore. "So we immediately moved Blass across from Seagram's Chateau in the States and put it into this company called Australian Benchmark Lines and things just started to rocket because we had our commodity product with Black Opal and then we had our premium brand with Wolf Blass. That gave our importers a range of products. Since then Wolf Blass has gone on to still be where it is and Black Opal's virtually disappeared off the

Wolf's a likeable, passionate man about what he does.

PETER PERRIN

market. So it's interesting that the brand integrity of Blass in the early days has no doubt maintained it to where it is today, while a lot of other brands have gone by the wayside."

Another great benefit was that Mildara was a well-run company, thanks to Ray King. This freed Wolf to do what he did best, travel and promote his own brand. "Mildara had these swag of brands that really didn't mean a lot, but they were a very well-run company," Peter says. "Ray King's a pretty smart operator, but he didn't have a hero brand and so the Blass brand fitted into that. And, while he didn't have an export business, he had a bit of cash."

Though Ray never really "got" Wolf, according to Peter, "He'd always say, 'Oh, Wolf's a bit crass.'" Ray was not interested in attending trade fairs, either. "If I asked him he'd say, 'Why would I want to do that? That's what you get paid for.' Whereas Wolf would be there and make an entrance and people would swamp him. I'd give him a gold pen and he'd sign bottles

for people all day. We'd almost got to the stage where he couldn't sign enough bottles and we considered getting a stamp made. But people didn't want that. They wanted the affinity with the man that was so successful with the product. I'm not saying that's the be all and end all, I mean a lot of other brands became very strong with export managers and whatever, but it was just that little bit extra that made the difference."

The determination to keep prices up and remain a premium brand worked well with the Canadian Liquor Board. "The reason that liquor boards control the retailing in countries like Canada and Scandinavia is to control alcohol consumption," Peter says. "Their charter is to not really grow in volume, but to control it. So the chance to make wine more expensive was fantastic to them. But sales actually kept growing and we had the largest selling wine and it was the most expensive wine." The Canadian system offers a general listing for

approved imports that means the product goes into every liquor retailing outlet in the country, and in 1989 it was offered to Blass at a price point under $CAD10. Blass said they didn't want that, asking instead for a specialty listing rather than having to drop the price. "That meant we'd be in a handful of premium stores, so we'd be in 10 stores instead of 1000. We held to that and finally we got a general listing at $CAD11.50." The Liquor Board told them nobody would buy Australian wine at that price. "And guess what? They did and it just kept growing," Peter says. It was also good fortune that the Canadian agents at the time handled prestige brands such as Bollinger, Absolut Vodka and Remy Cognac, so they understood premium brands. "So if you had a bottle of Wolf Blass on your table it must be good. It's like buying a Rolex or a Benz over a Holden," Peter says. "It's not whether or not the two things still do exactly the same job for you, it's the prestige element.

The Wolf Blass plant at Nuriootpa today grew from a piggery/tin shed (inset).

And we sort of use that analogy with Blass as an Australian wine. Of course, the quality still had to be there, I'm not saying it's all down to Wolf's marketing or my sales ability – certainly the guys making the wine knew what they had to do, and they were very good on that as well."

But with volumes hitting a massive 60 million bottles, would it be possible to maintain that famous quality, character and consistency of the house of Blass without the man himself at the helm? "I can absolutely guarantee it," Chris Hatcher says. Chris left Orlando, where he worked as a white-winemaker, to join Wolf Blass in 1987, specifically to learn about red-winemaking. His plan was to stay five years and move on. More than 20 years later, he was still there in 2009, as chief winemaker for Foster's in Australia and New Zealand, still working to the old Wolf Blass motto for winemakers, "no medals, no job".

"One of the great things with getting older is seeing young people come into the industry and add their dimension to it. I think the good balance that we've got at Wolf Blass now is that I have got the heritage of what Wolf started off, that experience, and I have got young people in the team that challenge and want to continually improve, and the blend of the two actually really works," Chris says.

"So you can actually keep things contemporary in style, but also over arch it with the house style that Wolf established. I think it is really important to be able to give them the background of the heritage and what Wolf was trying to establish, and also encourage them to make their own mark on where the brand will go in the long term. But in the end it's all about what's in the glass."

In a way the brand has already survived, even surmounted, the man. Staff talk about the day Wolf arrived at the winery to be welcomed by the temporary receptionist.

"Yes, can I help you?" It then became a comedy of misunderstandings as Wolf told her he was Wolf Blass.

"Yes, certainly, sir, you are at Wolf Blass."

"I am Wolf Blass."

"No, no, no, no, sir, the wine is called Wolf Blass. What is your name?"

As Chris Hatcher says, "I think that's a good indication of what the potential of the brand is."

Even without Wolf's relentless promotion, the wines continue to win medals, although they are now produced in such vast numbers. "We win more medals now than probably ever. For the last six or seven years we've been the most successful around the Australian shows, as a brand, by a long shot. That's important not just from a marketing aspect, which Wolf promoted a lot, but also as a driver for the team to set a level of 'we have got to achieve' and keep driving towards improvement. You have got to keep some incentive, you can't just keep tasting and sending them out and not getting a bit of feedback. It is easy to pat yourself on the back, but when someone else pats you on the back, that is really valuable," Chris says.

With all the setbacks and changes to distributors through takeovers it had been a tough job setting up the export success that is Wolf Blass today. "We had to jump major hurdles several times in Europe, the Americas and Oceania," Wolf says. "We were hit so hard that some industry competitors were actually feeling sympathetic about our bad luck. But we never lay down. This was the strength of the management of our brand."

"New World wines are mentioned all over the world and Wolf and John Glaetzer are responsible for that," Jim Murphy of Jim Murphy's Airport and Market Cellars in Canberra says. Jim, who supplies Australian wines to Canberra's embassies and sees first hand their international impact, says Chile and Argentina have followed the trail blazed by Blass and Glaetzer with the soft and approachable wines that they first produced and introduced to the US and the UK with their products from Langhorne Creek, the Barossa Valley and McLaren Vale.

The determination to establish effective international distribution was equalled by the lengths to which Wolf, and later Foster's, went to promote it. In fact, a lot of the things Wolf did back in the 1960s have been built on and adapted for modern-day campaigns. Although nobody today would dare consider some of the more outrageous stunts staged by Wolf and his mates in those early years. W

Wolf with IWSC Vice Presidents, Directors and Executives. Back row, left to right: Steve Hardiman, Executive; Frances Horder, Executive; Sir Anthony Greener, Vice President UK; Wolf Blass, Vice President, Australia; Baroness Phillipine de Rothschild, Vice President, France; Peter Duff, Executive Vice President; Bryan Hope, Honorary Vice President; Tony Salter, Director; David Wrigley MW, Director. Front row, left to right: Marchese Piero Antinori, Vice President, Italy; Peter MF Sichel, Vice President, USA; Jean Hugel, Vice President, France; Lord Thurso, Chairman; Paul Symington, Vice President, Portugal; Lord Montague of Beaulieu; Warren Winiarski, Vice President, USA.

Bottom: Wolf receives the Australian Export Hero Award from the Governor of Queensland, Her Excellency Ms Quentin Bryce AC in 2006.

Chapter 11

A GOLIATH OF A BRAND

Many of the great early Wolf Blass promotions were inspired by Wolf's involvement with friends through sport. It is a tradition that has been maintained by Foster's, although on a much larger scale, and probably without quite the same quirkiness. Wolf fears some of the fun has gone out of things these days. Certainly, it's difficult to imagine corporations getting up to some of the tricks he and his mates designed in the early days, including the creation of the slogan that has lasted throughout all the changes to the company.

"I need a slogan on my wines. They're quality wines," Wolf said to John Gordon one day when they were out on the ill-fated *Duplex 2*.

"No fish were biting and the wine was flowing, and I don't know how many bottles we drank before we came up with 'quality, character, consistency'," John says. "But, anyway, that's how it was created."

One of the first headline-grabbing promotions Wolf was involved in stemmed from his membership of the Barossa Valley Car Club. Adelaide businessman Charles Schmidt, the father of sparkling wine dispensing equipment in Australia, came up with the idea of promoting new products by serving them through petrol bowser-style tanks. While it didn't exactly set a trend for cars to be fitted with stainless-steel wine tanks as well as fuel tanks, it was certainly a lot of fun. Another crazy promotion involved an Elliot Ness-style team dispensing sparkling wine out of fake machine guns.

Wolf Blass with the first ever Melbourne Cup, won by Toryboy in 1865, which he bought privately. "Since I couldn't win one, I bought this trophy."

In 1986, Wolf organised a 30-minute breakfast program on the satellite channel Sky to promote a middle-market price point with the Red Label 1986 Shiraz Cabernet Sauvignon. It was beamed throughout the country from the hot and thirsty South Australian mining town of Coober Pedy, where houses are built underground and drinkers are enthusiastic. Around the country, tastings were held in pubs and clubs, anywhere that had a television set in a bar, and drinkers were offered breakfast. "That is how we approached the customers, and even those who preferred beer on the day probably would have tasted for the first time a red wine. It was a great bloody promotion and the Red Label took off," Wolf says.

In 1989, Wolf Blass Wines participated in the first International Wine Auction conducted by Sotheby's in London, with links to bidders in Europe, the UK and the US as well as at the Barossa Valley Vintage Festival. The Wolf Blass Special Pack of 88 bottles of red representing vintages from 1966 to 1987 sold for $6500, to Jack Roberts, then Queensland's leading liquor merchant. Wolf did a little pre-selling, though.

As chairman of that year's festival and an official Baron of the Barossa, he knew wearing the funny hat required of a baron would not be quite enough to get top dollar for his wines. "In order to get high prices, I had always some very good wine merchants behind me to bid for the products which I put up for auction. You could say

I rigged the auction, yes. That was all part of the excitement, to get the Wolf Blass name across."

Given his natural instinct for ensuring outcomes before going into events like this, it came as a bit of a shock when the organisers provided $3000 worth of wine locked up in the back of a wagon. Keys were distributed far and wide to bring people to the Valley to try to open the wagon's treasure chest. "We had huge publicity and, you wouldn't believe it, the first day when the vintage festival was on, somebody opened the lock. So immediately we had to replace the wine because that was a showpiece for the rest of the week, as far as the festival was concerned."

As an individual who began his own business with sheer passion and hard work, it has been difficult for Wolf to watch a major corporation take his name and grow it into a brand behemoth, and he sometimes regrets the changes to the way the business operates. "Innovative ideas by the young people aren't there anymore. As for me, I had all the pleasure to be part of all these things and of having business fun and having success at the same time. Unfortunately, these things have gone out of the door, the wind has blown out."

One of Wolf's great promotional successes involved his adoption of the bow tie. It was a practical choice, because long ties would get tangled in equipment when he was tasting from barrels, but it became a feature on his labels, in point-of-sale promotions and advertisements and on the widely read *The Entertainer* magazine

One of his great promotional successes involved his adoption of the bow tie, a practical choice because long ties would get tangled in equipment.

that was inserted into the glossy and inflight magazines. Wolf Blass Global Brand director Oliver Horn says promotions still reflect the way the man himself built the brand in the early days. It's just that the numbers are bigger and the event is international in scope. "It is a Goliath of a brand now, one of the most successful Australian wine brands in the world."

Wolf's discovery in the 1960s that Bilyara was the Australian Aboriginal word for eagle in his part of South Australia has turned out to be one of the greatest marketing tools ever sprung from a simple piece of anthropoligical research. As well as providing a fitting connection to Germany (the Eagle is the core of the German national crest), it also created a unique icon that consumers around the world associate with Wolf Blass wines. The Eagle inspired products such as the Eaglehawk and Bilyara ranges and is

dominant as a crest on every bottle, perched in a golden nest of grapes and vine leaves. It has been the centrepiece of every marketing campaign for the past 10 years. Today, the music from the TV commercials is so iconic that 95 per cent of wine drinkers recognise it. There are whole fan groups on the Internet and it can be downloaded as a ring tone. His winemaker John Glaetzer used to refer to it as the "golden chook", and certainly it has produced some mighty big golden eggs for investors over the years.

Although relative newcomers to the long story of Wolf Blass wine, Foster's have taken it to levels of growth that could not have been contemplated even by its exuberant founder. Until 1996, Foster's was a leading beer-only business and, as a company looking to accelerate growth, it acquired Mildara Blass to get a foothold in the wine market ,which was showing healthy returns and long-term growth potential. Mildara Blass

"No fish were biting and the wine was flowing, and I don't know how many bottles we drank before we came up with quality, character, consistency," John Gordon says of the now-famous standard.

Promotional postcard devised by Wolf, showing his sense of humour, punning on the word 'board'.

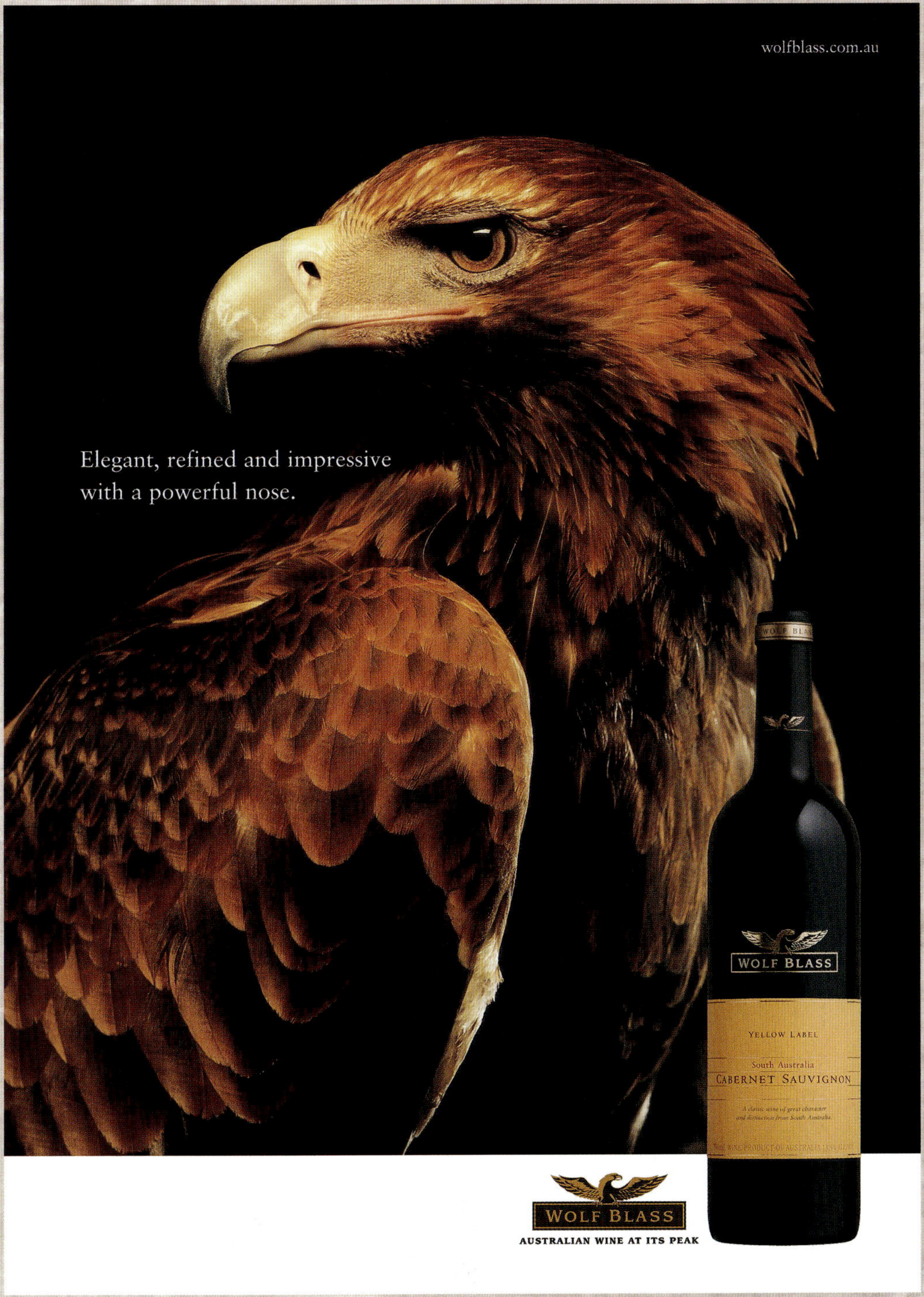
wolfblass.com.au
Elegant, refined and impressive with a powerful nose.
WOLF BLASS
YELLOW LABEL
South Australia
CABERNET SAUVIGNON
WOLF BLASS
AUSTRALIAN WINE AT ITS PEAK

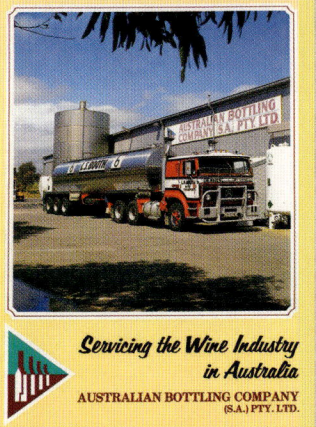

AUSTRALIAN BOTTLING COMPANY (S.A.) PTY. LTD.
Servicing the Wine Industry in Australia
AUSTRALIAN BOTTLING COMPANY
(S.A.) PTY. LTD.

The eaglehawk has been the centrepiece of every marketing campaign for the past 10 years.

was Foster's first wine acquisition, and the launch platform for subsequent acquisitions, mergers and buy-ins that have made it the world's largest wine company.

With that first purchase, the aim was clear – Wolf Blass was going to be Australia's No.1 brand, which it is. In 1994, the brand was selling six million bottles worldwide. In 2009, Wolf's 75th birthday year, it was selling more than 60 million. While Mildara Blass was bought initially as a boost to the domestic business, it is now a leading global brand with 75 per cent of production

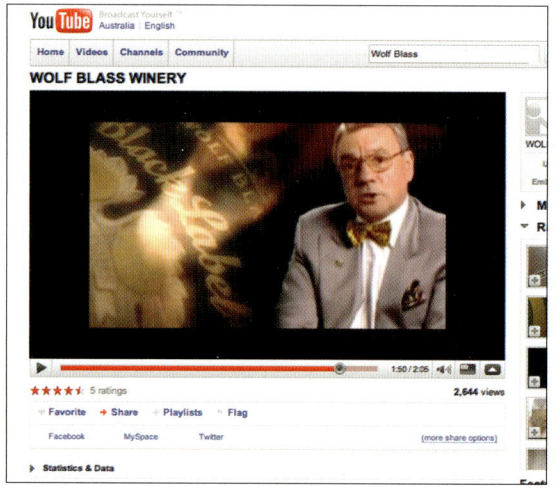

from the Wolf Blass Winery in the Barossa Valley exported.

Foster's first move after purchasing Mildara Blass was to extend production facilities at the winery, still at the site of that first tin shed. "Wolf was ahead of his time with this, too," Oliver Horn says. "He found a spot which was logistically well connected to everywhere he needed to be

and which has had room to expand over the last 45 years. We didn't need to vacate that spot, we could just grow and grow and grow, because he had already thought ahead. The street network and the connections to the infrastructure were already there and he thought, 'You know what? I build my winery there (my little shed) and I can grow further', and he has. He was ahead of his time, he was a good marketer and a good business man and we are still benefiting from that today."

Foster's has also continued with Wolf's inspiration in grading his labels by colour to make it easy for consumers to differentiate between wines, something he began in 1966 with the Yellow Label Sauvignon Malbec. In this case, Foster's has actually taken the label back to its beginnings, repackaging it with the original vine leaf and gold emblem.

Regular Wolf Blass consumers are familiar with the concept that if you want an entry level wine around $10, you look for Eaglehawk. Next is the Wolf Blass Red Label then Yellow Label, found in most grocery and wine outlets. The more premium level starts with Gold Label and then Grey Label and White Label, both at $30-$40. At the luxury level is the Jimmy Watson Trophy-winning Black Label and the even more exclusive Platinum Label. The company is also staying with the founding philosophy that wine should be made so people can drink it immediately if they don't have a cellar. "Wolf's founding philosophies of drinkability and making wine so people can drink it right away without having to cellar, the quality, character and consistency, are as true today as it was when Wolf really started out. So while it is significantly bigger, the values of the brand haven't changed," Oliver says.

In 2000, Foster's launched a 12-month television campaign, the first modern brand to do so. It also developed a strong alignment with sport, something Wolf had always done, particularly with ground signage. Although the expenditure was considerably greater compared with Wolf's first, wily attempts.

The man who hates to waste money simply propped a Wolf Blass sign on an A-frame on the back of his utility and drove it round the race track so that the cameras following the horses could not avoid filming it. "He caught on very early, because obviously he liked the horseraces, but also the iconic performance aspect of sports and that has always been represented in the brand," Oliver says. "It is the only one that has won four Jimmy Watson trophies, which has been named International Winemaker of the Year, twice, in 1992 and 2002 , internationally awarded Best Australian Producer in 2001 and the 2008 International Red Winemaker of the Year. So it is really one of the iconic brands of Australia, and iconic sports performance has always been a part of that, even to the point where, in the UK, we are the official wine of the Ashes grounds. Everywhere you see Wolf Blass signage on the

perimeters, and we are sampling Wolf Blass in the stadium."

And there is the man himself. "Everytime when Wolf Blass the man is part of an event, it just draws a significant audience," Oliver says. "There are not very many brands where the actual founder is still around and active in supporting the brand, and we have rolled him out around the world. He helps represent the brand at everything from black-tie dinners in Ireland to taking the Presidency at the International Wine and Spirit Competition in London or being interviewed on

Wolf Blass holds the ultimate global wine trophy, named after Wolf Blass, the man. With him is Rafael Guilisasti, the President of the International Wine & Spirit Competition, in London, November 2008.

In 1992 with
Shirley (left and
above) and his
co-owners after
Grooming won the
Brisbane Cup.

Horse trainer
Leon MacDonald
with jockey Claire
Lindop.

Some years after they'd been together, Shirley Nyberg-Blass bought a racehorse she called Brave Decision, because that was what she'd made when she decided to marry Wolf. It won the 2002 Darwin Cup.

Winning the twelfth Kangaroo Island Cup in 2004. "He gets as much pleasure out of winning a race at Clare as at Melbourne."

Wolf celebrates winning the Blue Ribbon Group One 1000 Caulfield Guineas with Dashing Eagle.

Asian television. He is the personality and the authenticity that many other brands just lack."

As an enthusiastic racehorse owner, one trophy that had eluded Wolf, and that he had long dreamed of winning, was a Group One horserace. In Australia, there is one race that every owner, every trainer and every jockey aspires to win – the Melbourne Cup, known as "the race that stops the nation" because when it is run on the first Tuesday of every November it's almost un-Australian not to care, even if you don't bet. Millions are spent on the day with bookmakers and betting agencies and the race dominates news coverage for weeks in the lead-up and then the let down afterwards. So, naturally, Wolf wanted to have a Melbourne Cup. But, given the odds, he accepted that he might have to get hold of one by some means other than owning the winning horse

He had fallen out with the trainer Bart Cummings, who has prepared more Melbourne Cup winners than anyone and is revered as a genius in racing circles. Wolf's need to be in control met an immovable force in Bart. "Bart got fed up with Wolf," recalls Peter Rosenberg, a racing colleague of Wolf's, one of the so-called "Nuri boys" from Nuriootpa, home of Kaiser Stuhl. "He said, 'Wolf, don't you tell me how to train horses and I won't tell you how to make wine.' So Wolf took all his horses away from Bart, but I still think they respect one another."

Wolf and Bart did have one big success before the split. It was in 1974, when a two-year-old, Ein Prosit ("cheers" in German), won the Breeder's Plate at Randwick in Sydney. The horse was jointly owned by Wolf, winemaker Brian Barry and businessman John Gordon. Wolf was in California, but had left instructions, he thought, to put $500 to win on Ein Prosit. When the horse came in first, he celebrated big time, thinking he'd won $1500. But the others had decided the horse was not a big chance and only put on $15, something Wolf seemed to hold Bart responsible for because of the advice he had given the owners. Five years later ,when Bart had another horse, Century Miss, to lease, Peter tried to put together a Nuriootpa syndicate. Wolf wasn't interested. "We finished up winning the Golden Slipper, so we had a great Group One winner before Wolf did," Peter says.

Still, Wolf wanted that Melbourne Cup and, if he couldn't win it, he would buy it. He was in London receiving the award for the International Winemaker of the Year in 1992 when he heard a Melbourne Cup trophy had failed to reach the reserve price at auction. He bought it privately for $121,000. It was the trophy commissioned for the Cup won by Toryboy in 1865. "Since I couldn't win one, I bought this trophy, which is an extremely important piece of Australian heritage in a race that has become an institution on the Australian calendar."

Wolf has loved horses since he was a small boy helping neighbouring farmers, and even considered becoming a vet. But he says he is not personally involved in the care of his racehorses. "The only hands-on I have got is to put my hands in the pocket to pay for the things. I have been in breeding, I do a lot of studying of the pedigrees and I am really up to date. I

take it seriously, because there is a lot of money involved. I haven't been successful in breeding, but I would think the majority of breeders wouldn't be. If we knew what A plus B brings, then everybody would make some money. But there is no money in it, really, in the long term, except that you need money to maintain an

He is a trophy monger.

FRED VELLA

interest in this sport." Wolf estimates he has lost a couple of million dollars on flesh purchases, excluding gambling expenses. He has been unlucky, despite a good eye for horseflesh.

One of his most unfortunate purchases involved a New Zealand horse called Synski . "He thought he could make a big business deal out of this one. But it wasn't very fair the way it went," his old Adelaide friend Fred Vella says. The horse ran well in two races before Wolf bought it, but he wasn't told that it had hoof rot. Unable to race it, he sent the horse to stand at Kangaroo Island and bought two of the first foals for about $7000. One of the foals, Barossa Boy, was sold to Western Australia and ended up winning more than $1 million in stake money. "That was a lot of money 20 years ago, and Wolf spent $7500 to buy it, prepared it, put it in the sales, got $7500 back and then the next bloke got over $1 million. And I honestly don't think he got one service fee from that horse. That was Wolf's going into the 'breeding business.'" Like all racing men, Fred and Wolf still think Lady Luck will turn anytime soon. "Not that he wants the money, he just wants to see the result. He is a trophy monger."

"I would think I had as much frustration as I had fun," Wolf says. Anyone who has watched Wolf's face and body language when one of his horses loses knows just how important winning is to him, in this as in everything else. "If I have got a horse winning, I am definitely over the moon. It is just a great kick."

The ten years up to 2008 were not great ones for Wolf on the track and he thinks his disappointment is deeper because he did so well in the previous decades. "I think this had something to do with being spoilt in the 1970s and then the 1980s, and probably the 1990s, when the competition wasn't as strong, and I had a very, very good relationship with a trainer called John Riggs, who was a personal friend. We would have had over 220 winners together." All up, Wolf's horses, wearing his racing colours of brown with a golden eagle, notched up 380 wins, including two Group One winners, Dashing Eagle in the 1000 Caulfield Guineas in Melbourne and Grooming in the Brisbane Cup. Dashing Eagle also won in a dead-heat in the Group One Flight Stakes.

Max Basheer met Wolf in the 1970s through John Riggs. Max regards Wolf as a good judge of horseflesh and the pair have owned a lot of horses together. "He's a very generous man, Wolf, not only with me but with everyone. He likes you to be involved with him and he enjoys your company and the feeling's mutual. He gets as much pleasure out of winning a race at Clare [a small country race club] as at Melbourne."

On his 60th birthday in 1994, Wolf established the Wolf Blass Foundation with a gift of $1 million and since then it has funded education and research and promotions in the wine industry. "The industry has been good to me and I would like to give something back." The foundation's first big event was in 1996, the inaugural International Wine and Health Conference. Epidemiologists from around the world discussed whether, medically, wine was just another alcoholic beverage. "This is the thing which the industry has to be fighting in the future at all times," Wolf says. "Alcohol will be under the knife if we don't separate alcohol from wine, otherwise it could be seen like the tobacco industry."

Another ongoing project of the foundation is a joint venture with the National Wine Centre, commissioning interviews with more than 180 icons of the Australian wine industry. The original interviews, conducted by historian Rob Linn, have been lodged with the State Library of South Australia and are the basis of a history of the industry by wine writer Max Allen. WB

Wolf loves his sport and sponsors many sporting events. Above: Wolf Blass rugby sponsorship with former Wallabies captain, John Eales. Right: Wolf, as ambassador of Adelaide Crows Football Club with Aussie sporting icon and AFL legend Ron Barrassi, Allen Aylett and his wife Marg.

Wolf Blass are the official wines served at Old Trafford, the homeground of Manchester United. Left: Wolf and United's long-time manager, Sir Alex Ferguson with Wolf Blass Global Wine Ambassador, George Samios (left). Wolf wanted to talk about soccer, Sir Alex about wine. Both wanted to talk about horseracing.

Adelaide football fraternity: Alan Sheppard, Steven Trigg, Max Basheer and Bob Hammond.

Norwood Football Club luminaries with Wolf: Nerio Ferraro, Denis Brion and Joe Tripodi in 2009.

Wolf Blass is one of the iconic brands of Australia, and iconic sports performance has always been a part of that. Left: Wolf Blass were sponsors at the 1996 Atlanta Olympics.

Wolf with Australian F1 champion Mark Webber.

Chapter 12

WOLF AND WOMEN

W olf loves women, anyone who knows him will tell you. "Wolfie loves women and wine and racehorses, but first comes the women," his younger brother Fritz says. But while his male friends talk about his enthusiasm for everything blokey, from cars to racehorses, pistol shooting and football, the women in his life speak of a different, quieter, more troubled Wolf. Certainly, a good way to try to understand the depth of a man's heart, the secrets of his soul and the extent of his fears and dreams, is to ask an ex-wife. She's moved on, but she will have seen him not just as an intimate partner, but also from a distance. She has judged him as lover, husband, friend and father.

Wolf has married three times and he does indeed adore women. He courts them, flatters them, buys them flowers and wine, regards them as excellent employees, and was known in his younger days for a tendency to lay a friendly hand on their persons, even if he didn't know them all that well.

Before feminism took hold, most women used to giggle and not take offence. The baker's wife at Nuriootpa, Jan Linke, remembers a young Wolfie chasing her around the kitchen table "just for devilment". Between the wives, he had girlfriends and, during his first two marriages, his wives expressed concerns about his roving eye. Not that Wolf necessarily saw it as a problem.

When asked in his 75th year about his predilection for politically incorrect behaviour – there are quite a few stories about Wolf's somewhat brash

Wolf Blass and his wife Shirley Nyberg-Blass in 2009.

Jan Linke, the baker's wife at Nuriootpa, pictured with husband Brian, recalls Wolf chasing her around the kitchen table, 'just for devilment'.

approaches at times to the opposite sex – he looks embarrassed but deals with it, regardless, with the frankness that has won him headlines for years. "Probably I have been very blunt, but I was just as long a bachelor as I was a married man. Yes, I've probably made a lot of faux pas. The faux pas – did I get punished? Yeah. Did I enjoy the punishment? Yeah. Did I have fun? Yeah. And I don't think there is anything wrong with that. I can say now that I have probably mellowed down and have become probably a little bit of an enchanter with a European touch."

As he also points out, women were his target market from the moment he arrived in Australia and began blending sweet bubbly wine and, later, soft, mellow reds and fruity, spritzy whites in the face of the sharp whites and big, butch,

tannin-laden reds that dominated the domestic market at the time. "I personally always thought that women are part of a lifestyle to make and bring happiness and I always enjoy beautiful women. I would have never made my profession what it is without them. My marketing and production and styles of wine – sparkling wine, Champagne styles – were all geared to get the opposite sex to enjoy this part of the lifestyle."

RAELENE

When her girlfriend Delmar organised a blind date with Wolf Blass, Raelene asked her if she would go out with him. "Not on your life," her friend replied.

It was 1965, Wolf was 30 and Raelene was 23. They got engaged in 1966 and married in 1967 in a double ceremony at the Adelaide Registry Office with Delmar and her boyfriend Fritz. Susan Blass was born in 1968, Sharyn in 1971. They divorced in 1975 after a couple of years of separations and reconciliations.

As Raelene herself says, she knew what she was getting into. But both were young and poor, Wolf living in Adelaide in a room with an Italian family, the Andelfottos, and Raelene sharing a house behind a dress shop. Years later, she is reluctant to say much about their marriage and refuses to say anything harsh about Wolf. They remain friendly and Raelene is a regular at family functions and all of the big birthday celebrations he has held every decade since he turned 50. "People can't always understand that but, hello, we've got two kids. Maybe there was animosity on my part to start with, but I got over that."

Wolf, on the other hand, is almost brutally frank about their relationship. "I don't think it was anything, really, what you call strategically planned. I think it was more or less, 'Look, I'm bloody working hard and you're working hard, why don't we get together, why don't we have a go?' You know, you talk about marriages of great emotion and everything, but it was, at the time, two people going to get together and see how we can get the thing going. And it just didn't really go. It just didn't work. It wasn't what you'd call a mastermind of a bloody great marriage. But we got two lovely girls."

In 1965, Wolf bought a home for them both in Adelaide, in Selth Street, Hendon, and worked on it in his spare time, and things seemed to be going well. "So we mastered something during that period," he says. "We grinded along and then it was, 'I think we should get married and have a baby. And then the first girl came and the second girl. But I don't think it was a marriage in heaven. It was just to complement each other, I think that's the way I saw it."

Wolf might say there was no great emotion, but others saw it differently. Margaret Lehmann knew them both well, swapping maternity clothes with Raelene, and she and her husband Peter got together often with the couple. She recalls dinner parties with the Blasses very clearly. The first issue was where to seat them. She worked out, eventually, that it was a mistake to put them at opposite ends of a dinner table. "Because then they would have a big fight and you'd realise it would have been better to put them near each other because then they'd at

In those days it was easier for a man to get and keep a job if he was married with a family ... It was seen as making him steady.

RAELENE KEMP.

least only shout softly." (The Lehmann's went to Wolf's first two weddings, but when he married Shirley in 1998 they weren't invited. "Shirley and I thought about it and we thought that you were a bad omen," Wolf told Peter.)

Wolf was definitely not the perfect husband. His and Raelene's second child, Sharyn, was due about the same time as the annual AFL grand final trip to Melbourne organised by the Nuriootpa Football Club and, while the doctor had suggested the birth was still days away, Sharyn arrived that weekend. It didn't go down very well with Raelene, according to Jan Linke. To be fair, this was an era when men were not expected to be hands-on dads, and they certainly were not made welcome in the labour wards, either.

"Yes," says Wolf, "I feel remorse. But after the event I was delighted that mother and daughter were in great health and the whole team celebrated. If Sharyn had been a boy we would have named her Peter, after Peter Hudson from Hawthorn, who was just short of the goal-scoring record."

As well as embracing with both hands the great Australian male tradition of drinking with your mates, marriage was also another way for Wolf to fit into his adopted country. "I'm not saying that's why we got married," Raelene says, "but in those days it was easier for a man to get and keep a job if he was married with a family,

because it was seen as making him steady."

Wolf also decided to get naturalised – "neutralised", as he called it. Given his childhood memories of being bombed by the British, it was a difficult decision. Wolf says initially he baulked at giving his allegiance to the Queen, although these days he's a monarchist through and through.

In the early days, Raelene would visit the winery a couple of times a week to do the books or write cheques. Looking back, Wolf thinks it is always a mistake not to include a life partner in your business. But both were also products of their times. Few people lived together before marriage in the 1960s, there was no childcare available and many thought that a woman's role was to stay home with the children.

The breakdown of Wolf and Raelene's marriage in the 1970s coincided with an economy in full swing that was taking women into the workforce in unprecedented numbers, and a feminist revolution that was telling women they could have more emotional and financial rewards from life than what was offered by the traditional careers of homemaking and childcare.

During their marriage, Wolf was working harder and harder as the years went by, with weekdays and weekends spent at the winery. Later, the building of a bar and a barbecue meant he could enjoy some sort of a social life at the same time. So when your husband is rarely home, not even for the arrival of your child, this message would have resonated strongly with Raelene, still then only in her early thirties. "Looking back, I don't know whether really he ever wanted to be married. I don't know. We just sort of went along and it happened," she says.

Wolf's father visited from Germany and stayed with them in Adelaide for three months in 1966. He was disappointed his son did not get married while he was still in Australia. "His father was lovely, a thorough, thorough gentleman." Raelene says. Every Tuesday, they went to a German restaurant for lunch and shared a bottle of Queen Adelaide white wine (Raelene had never drunk wine before she met Wolf). She would stay in town and put old Mr Blass on a bus with a note for the driver on where to let him off. He never saw his Australian grandchildren.

MARTINE

When the wealth began to arrive in the 1980s and the back-breaking physical slog eased off, Wolf was married to Martine Barrie, who was 20 years younger than him. They met during the 1978 Melbourne Cup carnival. It was the Sunday after Derby Day and Martine was having lunch with two girlfriends before flying back to Sydney, where she worked as a teacher of gifted children. "He was at the next table and very much the European. He sent wine over and it was obvious that he wanted to join the table, which he did towards the end of our lunch."

Flowers and phone calls followed and several weeks later the man himself turned up on Martine's doorstep with a single rose, a bottle of Chanel perfume and an invitation to lunch. For a 22-year-old convent-educated schoolteacher, the daughter of a strict German mother who was widowed when Martine was young, there was probably never any chance she could resist the flattering attentions of an apparently wealthy and by now famous man with a steely determination to achieve whatever goal he set himself. In this case, Martine.

Wolf proposed to Martine on her 23rd birthday, in March 1979, when he flew her to Adelaide to have dinner with a large group of racing friends, including jockeys and trainers. "He proposed in front of the whole table, presented me with the ring and rang my mother. They were babbling on in German like they were negotiating some sort of price for my head." Every mother-in-law joke ever heard might be applied to the relationship between Wolf and Martine's mother. "Often, being with the two of them was like being in the middle of a civil war because they both had egos, they were both opinionated and obviously quite Germanic in their approach to things, which, if anyone knows a German, they are organised to the point that it's exasperating being in their company sometimes, and exhausting. So I met Wolf and felt immediately quite comfortable. But between my mother and Wolf, I was the pawn. Wolf would say to her, 'What you must now realise is, she is now my wife.'"

After the wedding and the reception at the Tanunda Motel in the Barossa Valley, the newlyweds went to Kangaroo Island for the annual Kangaroo Island Cup. "I spent my honeymoon with John Riggs, the trainer, and a couple of jockeys and we all sort of bunked in together in one room at the Ozone Hotel," Martine says. It was to be the start of a new life filled with mutual friends and social occasions, and one which Martine enjoyed.

She was happy to budget with the $60 Wolf put in a cigar box for her every fortnight, but soon realised that a convent education and teacher training had not actually prepared her for home duties, especially cooking. So she bought some cookbooks. With Wolf's children at home on holidays and weekends, it was a skill she needed to acquire quickly. Wolf taught her his way to make a family-sized pot roast.

Thrift came naturally to her, inherited from her mother, and this suited Wolf's nature also, a man who, to this day, despite his wealth, likes to keep track of household accounts. "I respected him for it. And, really, at that stage in the early 1980s the wealth was all on paper, so we lived very modestly in his little Sturt Road house in Nuriootpa, with a green Perspex carport and the orange velveteen sofa and the light bulbs without shades.

"When my mother first came to visit us in that house she walked around and she looked at this light, just a cord with a bulb at the end of it, and she'd say, 'You've come from our home in Dover Heights [an upmarket Sydney suburb] to this. You've spent four years at university to drive that utility with an eagle on it.' Wolf would say, 'What's the point of putting a fitting on that bulb because eventually we're going to move and it will be $30 wasted.'"

These were by far the happiest days of the marriage, the ones Martine holds dearest. "There was an easiness. Wolf's friends were my family. We would dress up and have funny dinner parties and I'd dance on the table. But then all of a sudden he's a corporate man and that frivolity, the fun component of our life, was gone."

Until she had Anton, at 28, Martine travelled overseas with Wolf and was involved in the business in a number of ways.

"Johnny Glaetzer would take me into the lab and give me lessons in various aspects of winemaking and there was talk of me going to Roseworthy [the South Australian wine college] because, obviously, attending dinners and going to functions, I had to have a vague grasp of the industry. The wine industry was romantic and because it was very family orientated in those days there were all these wonderful personalities and characters and things. It was enticing."

When the money really began rolling in,

The two most influential people in my life are my mother and Wolf.

MARTINE BARRIE

Martine set her heart on buying Elderton in Tanunda, the old Tolleys house, and restoring it to its former glory. Bob May said, "No, she'll turn it into the Great Gatsby." Wolf said no because the property only had shiraz grapes and there was a glut of shiraz at the time. Bob was concerned about the expense of renovation and Wolf, despite his personal flamboyance on the marketing front, was concerned about appearing too grand.

Bob May says he now regrets that opposition. "That was one of the mistakes we probably made. Martine was looking for a home in the Barossa and we didn't go on with it. I kept talking Wolf out of it, because the ideas were grandiose. But it would have been a good hobby for her. It might have done something there…"

In New Zealand on a tour with company marketing boss Mike Fallon, Martine was feeling too ill to enjoy drinking the wine she was promoting, something she had never had a problem with. She was pregnant and her involvement in the company was about to take a back seat. "Anton was not an easy baby. He screamed all the time. Well, he was Wolf's boy child …"

Martine was an anxious mother. Her own mother had died by then, she had no close girlfriends to share her worries with and Wolf had recently launched Wolf Blass Wines as a public company so was by necessity consumed by work and negotiating a distribution network with Remy Martin.

When Anton was not quite four years old, Martine left Wolf for another man, one who paid her more attention, although later the pair tried a reunion, for Anton's sake, during a family holiday to Bali. But it was too late and a satisfactory settlement was agreed. They have retained an amicable association, particularly because there is a child involved. Meanwhile, Wolf had met and been intrigued by the elusive Shirley Nyberg, mature, successful in her own right, independent – and apparently impervious to Wolf's determined pursuit using his full arsenal of charm, Champagne and flowers.

SHIRLEY

Some years after they'd been together, Shirley Nyberg-Blass bought a racehorse she called Brave Decision, because that was what she'd made when she decided to marry Wolf. They met in the late 1980s, Wolf immediately launching into his courting mode, but Shirley made it clear she wasn't interested. He did eventually win her over, and they lived together for a few turbulent years.

A lesser person might have walked away, but here is a woman who, early in their relationship, bought herself a big, strapping Andalusian horse, called Mozart, which she rode three times a week in dressage. "I love a bit of a challenge," she says. And, like all good riders, she has a light touch and knows when to keep the beast on a loose rein and when to pull him in. It works, probably because discipline is one of Wolf's favourite words and he applies it to everything in his life.

After a few drinks, however, in those early days his self-discipline on social occasions often fell victim to his enthusiasm, something that pushed Shirley to the brink, so much so that in a crowded bar one night she slapped him hard. "There was a girl dancing around the bar and he just couldn't stop himself, cupping her behind and being very suggestive and it was

really hurting me." There was also a boyfriend who was looking ready to punch Wolf. Shirley got in first. "I turned around and I just slapped him so hard across the face and everybody, the whole bar, just stopped dead. Wolf just went stone motherless white. He looked at me and he sulked and the next minute he came up and he said to me, 'You have just done yourself out of millions.'"

To which Shirley replied that he deserved another slap for saying that. "If you expect that I'm going to put up with that humiliation, you're barking up the wrong tree, so you better go home," she told him.

Shirley returned home later and apologised, and it was one of the few occasions when she saw Wolf cry. "I think you're the only woman that's cared enough about me to even do that," he told her. It was a turning point in the relationship.

Shirley remembers well the day when they first met, in 1985. "I went to the races with a friend who'd invited me and it was quite a nice day and a short little bow-tied man just came up (as he always did, you know, throwing his chest out) and the bow-tie got bigger by the minute. And he said to my friend, 'Who's this?'

"Wolf was still married, but his wife was overseas. I don't know the whole story behind that, but she wasn't here, anyway, and I think things were already shaky." Wolf asked Shirley to follow him to the bar, bought a bottle of

Champagne and instructed her to stay with it until he got back. "He just sort of took over. He had pinned me down with the bottle of Champagne and then left. He would have been running around putting bets on throughout the afternoon."

One of Wolf's horses racing that day was called Night Bachelor, and Shirley mentioned White Knight was also a good name. Wolf, never one to let a chance go by, said he'd like to be her white knight. "I said, sorry, had one, didn't need another one." For a man who hates to lose at anything, that would have been a direct challenge. He invited Shirley to the birthday party of a mutual friend that same night, but before they went to the party they stopped at his friends Fred and Yvonne Vella, who were minding Anton while Martine was overseas.

"The amazing thing was I grew up calling the Vellas 'uncle' and 'aunty', but I hadn't seen them for donkey's years," recalls Shirley. What she remembers most clearly from that day was the Vellas going into a bedroom and coming back with a baby boy. "Say hello to your son," Yvonne told Wolf.

"And he was only ten months old and I don't know what it was, but something in me just wanted to go up and hug this little boy who was without his mum and he was a gorgeous little kid," Shirley says. Later, Shirley snuck away early from the birthday party, not easy since Wolf had followed her around all night. "He was insatiable," she recalls.

The following Monday she arrived at her shop, called I am Woman, to find a bunch of red roses, with one white rose attached to a card that

Shirley and Wolf moved in together in 1990, but it wasn't until 1996 that Wolf finally proposed. "I thought it was actually about time by then, because we were in it for keeps," she says.

read: "Have a wonderful day, from the White Knight." Of course, Shirley was impressed. "It didn't take much to work out where they came from and I thought, 'Oh, wow, this is rather nice and quite charming.'" Wolf had tried to deliver the flowers personally, but couldn't find the store.

Shirley didn't see Wolf again for almost six months, when she went to the Darwin Cup Carnival with the same friend. "After that he seemed to pop up everywhere, every race meeting I attended he seemed to be there, and in different places. Wolf would always ask her out. "He wanted to take me for a drive in his Rolls Royce." Shirley's answer was she'd been there, done that, and didn't need to do it again. "I think he smashed it up soon after that, anyway, but that was just a ploy, that was a sort of 'come and look at my etchings' sort of thing."

Eighteen months after they met, Wolf finally found a way to break through Shirley's resistance. He invited her to join him in his box at Adelaide's Football Oval for a match between Norwood and Port Adelaide. As it was Father's Day, he told her to bring along her dad. "Knowing that my father would be rapt, as he was an avid Norwood supporter, how could I say no? Of course I was going to go." Shirley told her then boyfriend her plans and they arranged to have dinner as usual after the game, but he didn't turn up. Taking on Wolf

Blass was just too much for him to deal with. "It was finished. Over. Not that I ever thought it was ever going to go anywhere, anyway," Shirley says.

So she started dating Wolf, but there are times she'd prefer to forget. "He was a real little bugger for quite a while and I thought, 'Well, I am not going to tolerate this too long.' But I forgave him a lot because he was going through a lot of emotions and he had this little boy Anton who had been through a bit."

Also, things were happening with the company, with a $6.5 million purchase of Quelltaler and Wolf leading a major export push to North America and the UK. Wolf had also driven his Rolls Royce into a power pole, with a blood alcohol level above the legal limit. The pole was declared dead, the Rolls critical. Wolf was unhurt, except for his ego.

Shirley and Wolf moved in together in 1990, but it wasn't until 1996 that Wolf finally proposed – in front of a crowd of 80 friends, family and media representatives. That was when Shirley made her brave decision. "I thought it was actually about time by then, because we were in it for keeps." Shirley has three adult sons whom she adores, from her first marriage to Martin Bergin, who she met at age 15 at a Sunday school dance. She was engaged at 16, married at 17 and had her three boys, Paul, Michael and Darren, by age 21. The marriage lasted seven years and after that she

Shirley is beautiful, she's sexy, she's a great companion, she's independent, she's sharp and she keeps me bloody straight and honest. And we love each other.

WOLF BLASS.

raised the children as a single mother. By 1985, she owned a successful fashion boutique and was happily independent.

WOLF

Memories are tainted by the passing of years and are disputed by other parties. The scars that have healed can still be seen and felt and, after the wives have told their stories, it is only fair to hear from the man in the lives of these three very different women, the man who variously entranced them, ignored them and tried to control them. And yet he remains one of the most important people in their lives. In his 70s, with no more big goals to strive for in business, he has at last taken time to think about the personal relationships that were important to him.

At times when he had to run hard to keep his business growing, he lost sight of his personal needs and those of his partners, although he never forgot the needs of his children. If he had to be away for any length of time, he always took one or another of them with him, and he kept in touch almost daily.

Wolf believes in being responsible for every detail of his life and that includes the lives of his families. The failure of two marriages distressed him deeply, and he seems to have always felt responsible for not managing things better. "In partnership, if you haven't got control of 51 per cent, even in your private life, it will fail eventually and it is going to bite physically, mentally, in whichever capacity you are operating in," he says.

One of the toughest decisions he made about the writing of this biography was to include so much personal detail, as seen from the not-

I love a bit of a challenge.

SHIRLEY NYBERG-BLASS

always-flattering perspectives of his ex-wives and old friends. But, with typical thoroughness, he decided that their stories were part of his story and therefore must be included, even if he did not entirely agree with some of the things they said.

"The first marriage, sad to say, was probably part of a necessity, trying to have a companion while I was working under very severe hardship. I've got two lovely daughters, so that's alright, and I make sure there's no hardship attached to my ex-wife," he told historian Frank Heimans for the National Library oral history project.

"With the second one, because I was travelling overseas building exports, I came home and suddenly someone else was sitting in front of the doorstep. The sad thing is that Martine's second marriage blew up, because she's quite an attractive, intelligent woman. The good news is a lovely boy was born. I was not putting enough attention probably to a woman's needs. And then I made another mistake; you should actually put your partner into a working position within your own framework, which I didn't do. That would have probably helped in many instances, and solved a lot of problems. I think any partner should be occupied and not be bored. I think that is where, probably, I am blaming myself for what happened, for not succeeding."

Despite the initial hurt on all sides, Wolf has remained friendly with his ex-wives. "Because there are children involved, I think this is the way. Unfortunately, the children always suffer on this issue, because they can't understand what has happened behind the scenery. I hope I have got a good background with my children. I hope they understand what I have achieved and that I have never let anybody down in the whole family system. Put us all in one picture and I think we have to be almost a Picasso. But I believe that I have done the best possible for all parties concerned.

"They may look at me as probably 'the Godfather' of the family and I think, whatever they may do wrong, I hope I can bloody

Shirley with her three boys, from left: Michael and his partner Karla, Paul and Darren.

straighten things out. I'm like an Alsatian dog looking after everybody. I'm lucky now to have a family and, if there's a little hurt, then good old Wolfie is going to be the great provider for all of them."

Wolf described Shirley to Heimans as "a very independent woman. We have a great relationship, the chemistry works, everything is alright. She's beautiful, she's sexy, she's a great companion, she's independent, she's sharp, she keeps me bloody straight and honest, and we love each other." **WB**

Shirley's grandchildren, from left: Candice, Madison, Joshua and Taylah.

Chapter 13

HOW GERMANS CREATED THE AUSTRALIAN WINE INDUSTRY

Wolf Blass and John Glaetzer were palates fated to prosper once they had met – the excitable German newcomer and the local boy of German heritage with a penchant for catchy phrases like "no wood, no good" in explaining his enthusiasm, shared with Wolf, for oak.

The Glaetzers settled in the Nuriootpa in the Barossa Valley in 1888 after emigrating from Brandenburg, Germany, and were among the earliest recorded viticulturists in the Barossa and the Clare. Wolf had arrived as a young winemaker in a raw new country at a time when the culture was changing from a beer-drinking man's world, where women stayed in the kitchen and cooked and hardly anyone drank wine. He became very wealthy, yet in the process of talking to people for this book it is amazing to discover how he has retained old friends from the days when they were all poor.

He was lucky enough to arrive in a place in Australia that had a strong German culture, although it was somewhat frozen in the mores of 19th-century Lutheran Germany. English and Germans settled the Barossa in 1842, but the Germans outnumbered the rest considerably. The townships of the Barossa Valley tell the story of its heritage and read like a long list of very good wines to anyone familiar with the Australian cabernet, shiraz and riesling: Krondorf, Langmeil, Tanunda, Gnadenfrei, Hoffnungsthal, New Mecklenburg, Siegersdorf, Neukirch, Nuriootpa and Seppeltsfield.

Wolf Blass, 2008.

Lutheran schools and churches kept the culture and the language alive. Before World War II, the children learned German at their Lutheran schools, but internment during the war meant that a generation missed out. When Wolf arrived, he noticed how many people of his age spoke "pidgin German". On the weekends, people from Adelaide would drive to the Barossa to eat at the German restaurants. The most entertaining spot then was Horst Bottger's Wine Stuber, where Wolf celebrated his 40th birthday.

A drive through the Valley with Wolf brings memories pouring back. Here he points out where the Post-Kutsche Restaurant was, now it has a different name; there was the Brauerhouse in Tanunda and he remembers the Brauerhouse at Angaston. He thinks that was the one where they even went so far as to wear lederhosen.

When he arrived, Wolf, as usual, threw himself into the social life, but realised there wasn't much going on, especially between competing winemakers and their companies. Here the lessons of grandfather Otto's strategically gregarious lifestyle swung into play, and Wolf bought them all together at the Horse and Herring Club and other venues.

"People came over from Leo Buring, Yalumba, Penfolds. Then I organised, following the vintage, that the winemakers should bring their best wine to a tasting of what the vintage looks like. I made the laboratory available and I think the first one was at Tolley Scott & Tolley. And then other companies offered their places also. While I did this, there was a method in my madness. I wanted to see what they were doing. Because I was already geared up for wine-show entries. I wanted to know what was happening, but at the same time it made professional sense that we knew each other and we talked."

So they talked with Wolf and they talked about him, not always kindly, because he was cocky, he didn't fit in with the prevailing wine establishment. Even his wine didn't fit in because, initially, it was made for people with unsophisticated palates. Worse, it was made for women, unheard of at a time when sherry was referred to behind closed doors as "mother's ruin" and ladies did not drink, not if they were real ladies.

Not that Wolf was the first German winemaker in the Barossa Valley to make a little something for the ladies to drink. In 1955, Colin Gramp from Orlando offered Guenter Prass a three-year contract to leave his home in Germany to come and make Barossa Pearl sparkling wine. It was Orlando's success with this style of wine that led directly to Wolf being employed in Australia by Kaiser Stuhl.

The two men didn't meet until a few years after Wolf's arrival, but they have been close friends since. Guenter is a founding board member and trustee of the Wolf Blass Foundation: "Everybody on the board believes that it is a fantastic way for Wolf to repay to the country for his success and

Wolf Blass (foundation and life member of German Karnival Group) and John Glaetzer (Karnival Prince). "We hit the industry so hard, John Glaetzer and me, it became obscene," Wolf says.

we admire him for it. There are very few people who turn around and say, 'I'll give you a million dollars and see what you can do with it.'" But even in an industry well known for its great friendships between commercial rivals, there are always pockets of jealousy.

"Many things have been achieved, which perhaps have not been as recognised as they should be, but that's life," Guenter says. While it was not always fully appreciated in some quarters that Wolf turned the industry around from a small exclusive club to a mass market, by the 1970s most players at least realised he was on the right track. "Winemaking is important, but what's so good about having the best wine if you can't

sell it? Until the early 1960s, the winemaker made the wine and said, 'You better buy it because I made it.' Wolf, he was the first one to look upon it a different way, saying, 'Well, I'm here to serve the people, to serve them what I believe they want.' And he was right."

Both men were also early members of the local wine industry club, the Bacchus Club. Guenter remembers when Max Schubert brought along samples of his early Penfolds Grange. "Wolf was one of the first ones who said that was the wine of the future."

Even as competitors in the 1960s and 1970s, the two were close, with Wolf winning all the prizes for red and Orlando, with Guenter as winemaker, the

Wolf as Baron and PR Director with Vintage Festival queens in 1973.

most successful overall exhibitor in the major wine shows. "We got closer together and we exchanged views, so it was very nice," Guenter says.

Canberra retailer Jim Murphy was also impressed early in his career by Wolf's willingness to be a mentor and to share with others. It was Jim's idea, when he was beverage manager of the Staff Club at the Australian National University in the capital, to get Wolf involved in what turned out to be a major seminar, the first of its kind, into the wine industry in Australia.

Here, in 1979, about 400 people from all segments of the wine industry came together to share their trade insights. "Up until then the industry was quite secretive," Jim says. "I was just 21 years old when I met Wolf and from then on I would phone him a couple of times a year and he would tell me exactly what was going on, and very honestly, from any part of the industry's point of view."

Wolf also encouraged Jim to leave his steady job at the staff centre and launch his own, ultimately very successful, business. "He said, 'Just do it and I'll support you.' When you work for institutions and you get super and holidays and all of a sudden you give all that up, you have to start believing you can do it all yourself. So to have someone to provide that extra crutch is unbelievable. I think he's done more for the Australian wine industry than anyone else. He's a wonderful man."

Despite some disapproval of his more outrageous publicity stunts, there were always people around Wolf who loved him enough to call him a friend, forgive him his impatience, his authoritarianism and blind determination to do it his way, even if it was just catching fish.

John Glaetzer used to go fishing on the river with a half dozen friends and they would usually be successful. Taking Wolfie with them was problematic. "We took him out gar [garfish] fishing one night. We would go out in the boat, a little tinnie, and we'd have a 10-foot handle with a ring on it and a wire net and an underwater light to see the fish. We'd just lob on the top and the fish would jump and you would put them in the boat. This night there were six of us on the boat and we came across a school of jumping mullet – the water is boiling and there is Wolfie knocking everyone arse over head with this big broomstick. So we are all ducking and Wolf is catching probably six or eight fish at a time. Instead of going into the boat he is tossing them out the other side, because he was so excited!"

John also tells the story of how Wolf discovered his natural talent for tasting. In 1967, while studying at Roseworthy College, at Wolf's suggestion he was doing some work at Normans, where Wolf was consulting as well as making his own wine. "It was during the vintage period and Wolfie lined up 17 red wines – all one year old – on the tasting bench. I had not tasted wine like that ever and Wolfie said, 'Glaetzer, you pick out your first, second and third.' So I went through and tasted them all and kept some notes and then

I wrote down the first and gave a reason, second and third, gave my reasons, and Wolfie wandered into this little lab and he is getting shitty because I am wasting time, because it took me an hour to do a five-minute job. Then he read my notes and then he got even more furious; he was jumping up and down and his head hit the ceiling because he reckoned that I had been looking at his notes, and as he is jumping up and down he pulls his own notes out of his back pocket and he couldn't believe it." The notes were almost the same, despite John having an untrained palate.

From that day, Wolf demanded that John come work for him as soon as he graduated. In 1970, he joined Wolf at Tolleys as assistant winemaker and within a year had followed him to his new winery, Bilyara. The partnership became one of the legends of the Australian industry. "We hit the industry so hard, John Glaetzer and me, it became obscene," Wolf says. Remembering his problems with Tolleys not wanting him to make his own wines, Wolf was happy for John to keep producing his own products, under the label John's Blend.

Cellar manager Chris Hausler joined Bilyara around 1978 and was aware of the blending skills that were needed to overcome some very ordinary grapes at times. "Johnny and Wolf, especially Johnny, performed a lot of miracles in those days. He hit a lot of crap. Johnny used to show his batch of barrels and then Wolf used to do his and they used to blend the current vintage, or the one-year-old vintage, with older wines to give a

John Glaetzer in 1999. Wolf was happy for John to keep producing his own products, under the label John's Blend, which today sells out every year, exporting to Switzerland, the US and Britain.

sort of a softer look about it, but pick the oakiness up. So they'd blend a little bit of this, a little bit of that with some special older material, put it on bentonite in the barrels [to take out the proteins] and that used to be the Jimmy Watson or their show entries for that year. Then there was always a competition to see who won."

Len Potts was one of the first vignerons to supply Wolf with the Langhorne Creek cabernet sauvignon and shiraz grapes that made his wine such a showstopper. Unlike the majority of early settlers, Len's great grandfather arrived from Portsmouth, England, on the sailing ship *Buffalo* in 1836, moving to Langhorne Creek in 1850 and growing his first grapes there soon after. The company today is owned and operated by fifth-generation members of the family and the winery is listed on the State and National Heritage Registers. Its Bleasdale wines are prizewinners and highly regarded. Len remembers going down to the vineyard with his father, pulling out gumtrees to plant more vines.

"We were sitting there one day on the bank of a big hole that was dug, where we'd grubbed this tree out, and he picked up a gum tree root and he was rubbing it in his fingers and he smelt it, he loved smelling things, and he said, 'You smell that. Isn't that like the red wine?' And it bloody well is. Langhorne Creek's got that peculiar ability that those flavours come out. Fennel is another one, it's a weed around here. And we still get a lot of chocolate out of Langhorne Creek wines." The chocolate was such a strong feature of the early Blass wines that John Glaetzer reckoned the judges would go through first and knock out all the chocolaty and eucalyptus entries, "because they didn't want Wolf to win any more".

Wolf is fairly scathing about some of the so-called Langhorne Creek wines sold today. "When we started, with the Bremer flooding, there was a different silt and soil structure, a different flavour. Today they have been planting the stuff bloody 30 kilometres away and do different areas and they are still calling it Langhorne Creek." The Potts vineyards are on those original rich alluvial soils that are flooded regularly, and when the floods come and the vineyard is isolated, that is when the great wines are born.

John Glaetzer and Len Potts looked at the years when Wolf Blass produced its top wines, including the first three Jimmy Watsons in his own name, and in each case they were related to the wet years in Langhorne Creek. "We grew crops, fairly indifferent ones, I suppose, in the dry years," Len says. "But John maintains they were always top quality, that he could always make good wine out of Langhorne Creek. It's just that the wet ones were the peak."

John has left Foster's, but he still makes his own wines, John's Blend, as he did when working for Wolf, and he still works with the Potts family. He is also in partnership with a fifth-generation Potts, Bill, and his son Ben, producing Gipsie Jack (named after John's jack russell, Gipsie) from Langhorne Creek. John's Blend sells out every year and John has been exporting for 25 years to Europe. Switzerland, the US and Britain, among others, are top markets for him in particular.

Today, for winemakers at the early point of their careers who want to put their own stamp on a wine – and make a living – this kind of operation would be difficult to sustain in the face of competition from global conglomerates. In 2009, with a worldwide wine glut in play, Wolf feared for the future of small companies in Australia, even though he felt they had more "heart" in their winemaking. He also believed there were too many different labels in Australia – probably as many as 35,000 – and too many individual winemakers clamouring to make their

names into a brand. Even the enthusiasm for wine- and food-focussed short-break holidays in the tourism industry could not keep every small winemaker in the country in business.

"Cellar door is something affiliated with the hospitality and tourism industry, so therefore I don't think you can make this a commercial point," Wolf says. "You have to have a brand to build on; if you haven't got the brand, you are struggling. We have individuals who like to introduce their personality on the label. Does it have any impact on building a brand? No, it's a dream. If you are going to be a solid, cash-flowing business with no debts in our industry in Australia, with 25-35,000 tonnes you are sitting pretty well, being competitive and making a good return. But there

aren't too many around." In 2009 there were about 2300 independent wineries in Australia, many of them looking for a point of difference by introducing grape varieties to try to get into restaurants. "My opinion is we should stick with what we know best and that is cabernet and shiraz, not merlot and not pinot noirs," Wolf says.

Smaller wine companies are also going to suffer as exporters drop their prices in the face of the global financial meltdown and a wine glut. "High prices are going to come down to a lower pricing structure and the smaller wine companies cannot afford to bring a low-priced wine on the market," Wolf says. Because they simply cannot compete with the discounted big-name brands offered by major retail chains, the small producers rely to

In 2006, the President of the Federal Republic of Germany, Horst Koehler, through the German Ambassador Martin Lutz (pictured) presented Wolf with one of the nation's highest awards, The Cross of the Order of Merit.

1978: Prince Karnival Wolfgang The First. Wolf Blass was a major sponsor of the club for many years. Wolf is a life member.

a large extent on restaurateurs and independent retailers keen to find new, well-priced brands. Wolf has always been opposed to selling his wines through discounters, but even his brand has gone the way of the chain.

"Chains don't allow you to build brands: you may be in today and you may be out tomorrow. You have to have money in order to get shelf space. The retailing structure has changed from where we were. We used to have independent, nice family retailing liquor stores, hoteliers."

At dinner one night in London with marketing manager Oliver Horn and one of Foster's biggest UK customers, Wolf espoused his views on discounting and discounters in his usual forceful way. "We had to pick up the pieces for a couple of months afterwards," Oliver says. "The reality is that Wolf Blass is the No.1 brand in Australia and you can't be the leading brand and not be in the supermarkets. And what the supermarkets do in order to be attractive and competitive is they obviously offer promotions for consumers and, while it lowers the prices, it also gets more of our wine into more consumers' hands."

Even Wolf would have trouble surviving and growing if he were starting out in the market conditions that have prevailed since 1990, when takeovers and acquisitions changed the face of the industry. He had to face the fact that his small brand could not survive alone when he merged with Mildara and he has not personally blended a wine since.

"When Mildara came in, they had different grape varieties, they used different vineyards, which we never had," Wolf says. "So there was internal turmoil and it almost broke the back of Wolf Blass Wines. Suddenly we had new winemakers coming in from the other side and we were just lost between, 'Is it to be about the Wolf Blass style or are we going to develop a new style and leave the Wolf Blass.'"

Wolf believes the winemakers employed by corporations today do not always have the freedom to create the best wine to fit consumer needs. "The more the marketing people are going to tell the winemaker what to do, the type of wine to be produced and the price it will have to be, the less he or she can concentrate on the final parts of where and how to go about doing a good job." But it is inevitable that this will happen because of the need to continually increase profits. "If growth is the only way you will be accepted by shareholders, then eventually it doesn't matter if you are a BHP, an AMP, a Qantas, a Ford or a General Motors, you are going to come somewhere to the end, because there will be a rationalisation, there will be somewhere you cannot go".

Wolf is staunch in his conviction that cabernet shiraz varieties are the national benchmark that differentiates Australian wines from those in other parts of the world . He doubts that new grape varieties can work in Australia. "I think we can make a wine which is different from 90 per cent of all other countries, except probably Chile and Argentina. But there is no comparison with the northern hemisphere, where there is a cold climate, higher acid and a different complexity. They have got different grape varieties; their pinot noirs are different from what we make, because we can't really make it. We should stick with what we know best, which is cabernet shiraz and shiraz – not a merlot or a pinot noir.

"The little winemaker is adopting new grape varieties because he wants to get into a restaurant. But, from a global point of view, it is not in our best interest, and without the global market we would be finished in this country. We in the southern hemisphere, we have got tools and our winemakers have got more flexibility than I think the people from the northern hemisphere. Unfortunately, we have got too many small wine companies and we have grown out of proportion because the so-called leaders of the industry have seen an increase in sales for 12 years and have never been in a position to see that one day sales are going to fall. The high prices are going to come down and the smaller wine companies cannot afford to bring a low-priced wine on the market. So the benefit today is that the consumer never had it so good."

By 2009, Wolf had been warning for several years that only a handful of companies would survive an over-supply of wine, and they would be those who standardised their products. With the global economic crisis in play, the situation became even more dire.

"Orlando is definitely one that will survive, then Lindemans, Blass and Penfolds. There is also a future for a few middle-sized family companies in Australia like Yalumba , Tyrrell's and Brown Brothers." Experience, a premium product and regular contact with loyal and longstanding customers will keep operators like John Glaetzer in business, whatever happens, but there is no question many will fail. "They're starting to fall over now, and not just the small ones." W

In others' words

For years, Wolf Blass believed himself unloved and unpopular among many of his peers, particularly those he regarded as Old Establishment. Yet, in 2000, when he was named the 10th recipient of the industry's most prestigious honour, the McWilliam's Wines Maurice O'Shea Award, the audience stood and applauded for five minutes. This home-country honour came on the back of a swag of international industry awards, not to mention almost 4000 trophies for his wines.

Global recognition first came in 1992, when he won the Robert Mondavi Trophy as International Winemaker of the Year at the International Wine and Spirit Competition (IWSC) in London. In 2000 and 2001, he was awarded Best Australian Wine Producer by the IWSC. In 2002, he was named International Winemaker of the Year by the IWSC, winning the Robert Mondavi Trophy for the second time. In 2004, he was appointed Vice-President of the IWSC and, in 2005, President and Lifetime Vice-President.

That same year, the Robert Mondavi Trophy was renamed the Wolf Blass Trophy. In 2008, Wolf Blass Wines won International Red Winemaker of the Year, the world's biggest wine competition involving the blind-tasting of 9000 wines.

If the standing ovation that night in Melbourne when he picked up the Maurice O'Shea ("in recognition of the enormous contribution he has made to the Australian wine industry") didn't allay any lingering concerns in Wolf that he was still regarded as an upstart outsider, the plaudits that followed – from critics, industry leaders and politicians – certainly should have.

'Talk to his contemporaries in the industry and they will cite his influence on winemaking and flavour. But they also speak of his generosity and dynamism, both with time devoted to young winemakers and with money to support the industry," wrote Sally Marden of *The Wine Magazine*.

Wine writer Huon Hooke said that Wolf was "a multi-talented fellow", and many believed his greatest success was in marketing. "By sheer force of personality, Blass created a brand that quickly became a household word. It's often said that marketing cannot be taught and the best marketers have an innate feel for the commercial world that cannot be passed on. This is especially true of Blass."

James Halliday wrote in *The Weekend Australian* that, "his spectacular success was due to an uncanny ability to predict public taste, a genuine commitment to quality and a marketing genius. May the man in the lurid suits and the virulent bow-ties never lose his passion or his appetite for life."

According to the then Premier of South Australia, John Olsen: "Wolf Blass may claim German origins, but we South Australians proudly claim him as one of our own. His contribution to and devoted nurturing of one of this State's most important industries is seen by many to be

Wolf Blass with former Australian Prime Minister John Howard celebrating the release of a fourth Jimmy Watson trophy winner at a fundraiser.

been generous to the core and given much back to help prosper the industry you love so much."

The plaudits continued to come thick and fast when the next year, 2001, Wolf was appointed a member of the Order of Australia in the Queen's Birthday Honours List. The little German boy who had watched British and Allied bombs dropping like Christmas trees on his homeland would never have believed it possible that he could not only receive an award from a British sovereign, but also declare himself a staunch monarchist.

Also with this honour came congratulations from some legendary names in the industry itself, such as Tolley, McGuigan and Angove.

There was also a message from the chair of the South Australian Jockey Club, Peter Lewis, who told Wolf: "If ever there is a humanities award for being a 'bloody good bloke' you would be the first recipient."

John Howard, the then Prime Minister of Australia, wrote to him: "It is a fitting tribute to your service to the Australian wine industry."

Many Australians would drink to that.

unsurpassed. His personal and professional achievements have been an inspiration to the industry." Olsen added that the establishment of the Wolf Blass Foundation, in 1994, typified the calibre of the man. "Wolf is determined to unselfishly foster continued industry excellence in viticulture, winemaking and marketing. I can think of no other person more worthy to receive the 10th McWilliam's Maurice O'Shea Award. It is an honour richly deserved."

The then CEO of the Winemakers Federation of Australia, Ian Sutton, said: "It is befitting that Wolf should be honoured with the Maurice O'Shea Award, the pinnacle of achievement in the Australian wine industry, and it is testimony to Wolf's drive, dedication, skill and passion for the advancement of the Australian wine industry."

David Brownhill, the chair of the Australian Wine and Brandy Corporation, told Wolf: "You have

Chapter 14

AFTER THE WINE DAYS

Mike Rann, South Australian Premier, and his wife Sache celebrate Wolf Blass's birthday with Wolf and his wife Shirley.

2008. A lively baby, a bossy toddler, a wild boy and a lifelong charmer.

Wolfgang Franz Otto Blass was in a hurry even before he was born. His mother Irmgard wanted to have the birth at her parent's home in Stadtilm. She and his father Friedrich were on their way there from Halle, where he was employed as an academic, but the baby took control and came into the world between the Saxony and Thuringia regions, in a small village called Sitzenroda, as stated in his passport. He's been in a hurry – and in control – ever since, with one or two exceptions that, at 75, still bothered him.

He was a lively baby, a bossy toddler, a wild boy and a lifelong charmer. He became a man who drummed to his own tune and, yes, not unpredictably, drumming is Wolf's preferred form of musical expression, whether on a drum kit, a handy table or bar. As a boy, when piano lessons were scheduled at home in the villa at Stadtilm, Wolf disappeared.

In 1996, with the Foster's acquisition, suddenly he had all this money in the bank, but nothing to do. His third wife Shirley had seen him through his life's traumas, business and personal, for many years (and with Wolf most things are either traumatic or triumphant). She suggested they buy a farm. "Shirley and me, we thought we need a little bit of something, a little bit more what you call farming or an outdoor interest, if we can get a beautiful block of land somewhere, which we did on Lake Albert [in South Australia, near the mouth of the mighty Murray River]." But before the small farm, Wolf first went into a big farm – deciding he

Wolf with his model railway set, 2005.

would get involved in building the biggest dairy farm in South Australia. He went into partnership with mining magnate Robert de Crespigny. "French," Wolf says, as if this is enough to explain his thoughts on the matter. Because anyone who knows Wolf knows it is a word he uses nearly always with negative emphasis.

Even more surprising, given his lifelong mistrust of the French and his troubles with Remy, was that he took a minority shareholding. "He had his partner and myself and a partner and, unfortunately, when we bought this whole complex and were developing it, here again the 51 per cent and 49 per cent was swinging the axe against the minority shareholders, which was me and James Harvey," Wolf says.

Bob May had cautioned against the dairy farm plan. "It wasn't de Crespigny's fault that it

all went pear shaped, it was just the timing. They had a shared vision, but they were two completely different cups of tea – chalk and cheese. De Crespigny saw a little before Wolf that it just wasn't going to make money and he's much more hard-nosed than Wolf and he cuts losses quickly and moves on. Whereas Wolf would think about it and ask, 'How are we going to deal with the people. Let's give it another go.' But we got out; we got some money, no question about that. I mean, he wanted to make cheese. You're never going to make money out of cheese." Cheese-making would have been a pleasant hobby in Wolf's mind, complementary to the wine in a way, but it had to pay its way.

Next, Wolf bought the smaller farm beside Lake Albert. Shirley organised the building of a magnificent stone cottage. "We enjoyed going over there on the weekends with the rubber boots on and we just did our thing." Then Wolf had an idea, and the rural retreat became another money-making project. This time it was about beef cattle ("you know, the black ones"). Aberdeen Angus were to be the new, new thing for farmer Wolf. "We re-fenced everything and we did the whole of it and we spent money and cultivated the land and then I had problems with the staff. With tears in our eyes we abandoned the project. I must say I enjoyed going there, it was really wonderful, there is no doubt about it – it was a masterpiece, because we worked on it all the time and I loved it." In the end, the venture would have failed of its own

accord, without the people problems that led Wolf to sell up, as drought hit South Australia harder than anywhere in Australia and led to increased salinity in Lake Albert.

He even considered, more than once, going into stud farming. "I looked very seriously, but then I said to myself, 'No, this is too dicey.' Shirley always said, 'Look, why don't you just leave it as fun?' But I said that we must get some return, somewhere, somehow, and that's why I tried to get into the beef business. Because this is my nature … that every time I am going to go to something, I like

to see some return. You have to give a busy man something to do, otherwise he is driving himself mad, and I couldn't stand in the kitchen with my wife 12 hours a day."

Wolf then looked at property development, getting involved in a land subdivision in Adelaide and then some property deals in Queensland. None of them worked out as well as he'd hoped, but he needed to be occupied and he had money sitting in the bank.

"He went into some foreign territory," Bob May says of his and Wolf's property dealings. "But he

Wolf Blass HQ in Adelaide. Wolf still goes into the office every day unless he's away. "It is a part of my life."

Governor of South Australia, Sir Eric Neal, presents Wolf with his Order of Australia in 2001.

as well as the wine promotions. "Operating in conjunction with the headquarters on the further development of the brand of Wolf Blass – I think I enjoy this. It is a wonderful, wonderful part of my life. All the global accolades which I have received have not been because I am sitting at home, but because I am moving about globally."

Yet Wolf has often said he dislikes publicity, doing it only for the sake of the brand. Sport is his relaxation. "There, everybody is equal, so you relax." Although, over the years, in Australia his most direct attempts at sport as relaxation haven't always been successful. If he went fishing, he nearly blew up the boat, almost turned it over or simply got lost. He holds a shooter's licence, but when Shirley started to outshoot him at target practice that interest waned. He's had success with his racehorses, albeit at a financial cost. And he may have been a member of the Barossa Valley Car Club for decades (and is a past secretary), but there's general consensus among friends and family that Wolf is a terrible driver because he has so much else going on in his head. He prefers to be driven these days.

Still, he is fit and athletic, was a good soccer player and is still a top skier and is a life member of at least ten sporting clubs, including the Victorian Ski Club, two football clubs and several horseracing clubs. He is a member of the Adelaide Pistol and Shooting Club and the Adelaide Shooting Club. At his gun club, each year he would take along two trophies to award to

was a punter, I was the pessimist. He would say there were some good people involved, they had money, he had money, so why not get together."

But Wolf hates failure and he hates being associated with people who fail. He is always quick to pull out at the first sniff of it and, somehow, between his optimism and Bob's caution, he keeps making money, even if it isn't as much as he expected. Eventually, he struck the right property, a shopping centre development in the booming upmarket South-East Queensland seaside resort town of Noosa. As Bob May says, he was able to learn from the early experiences and turn them around to great success.

But it still left a busy man without a plan for his days. So he returned to his beginnings – to Wolf Blass wine. In 2009, he still goes to the office every weekday unless he is travelling, and a staff of three are kept on their toes with one project or another,

When you go up the lifts and you sit up there on the mountain, you start going back and you start looking at people I had been affiliated with and they are already gone 10 or 15 years ago and I had to make the eulogy, then I think to myself, 'How lucky am I? I am still here.' You know, this is what goes through your mind, because you're in a different world up there and I am just saying to myself, 'This can't be true.'

WOLF BLASS

winning teams, a large one, in case he won, and a smaller one in case he did not. His team was the most consistent loser, until the year he recruited crack shots from the South Australian Police Special Forces division, and finally took home the big trophy with his name on it.

He talks about giving up some of his still very active involvement in the running and financial affairs of many of the clubs, but they're so close to his heart that it will be a wrench. He fears there's nobody else to do it properly.

Wolf also talks about spending more time with his family, although with his youngest, son Anton, in his mid-20s he might find they are busy with their own lives. Shirley continues to run her own property interests, separately. Occasionally, when driving somewhere, mostly in Queensland, where her grandchildren live, she'll point to a building and mention she owns an apartment there. "I think she's planning something right now," Wolf tells me as we farewelled each other after our final interview. Clearly, he knew better than to ask what it was.

He confided that he'd been in big trouble recently because, while he'd bought extravagant gifts for Shirley on Valentine's Day, he had forgotten to buy a card. After leaving me, he was off to buy a birthday card well ahead of her actual birthday, just to be safe. "When my wife is angry that kettle really boils and puts me in hot water."

She also has more insights into the private and personal side of Wolf Blass than anyone else. She says that, even after Foster's, Wolf's life didn't change dramatically. "The travelling didn't really slow down at all. In fact, in some ways being an ambassador for the brand put a bit more pressure on him; he's a man that if he has a job to do he feels really committed and will want to do his best and, of course, he has the fear of losing the recognition. And he needs recognition just like we need shoes to wear."

Yet at other times he'll shy away from people and company, disappearing into a quiet place at home to watch television, alone, usually the history channel. "He will watch war movies constantly, every night, anything to do with the war. But if it's something that's just a sad, emotional family story he has gone so far as to flick it off even if I'm watching it. He'll say the war

is real. And I'll say so are emotions. But Wolf will watch war almost every night of our life that he's able to watch television. Obviously, growing up in the war had a huge effect on him, knowing what it's like to be without, and I think he's always got that fear he could lose everything."

Wolf's biggest losses during the war were emotional rather than financial, because there was always food on the table and a roof over his head. His brother Fritz remembers his grandfather and mother and aunts trading schnapps and wine with the farmers for food. "All of us children, there were about ten of us, we had lots of freedom, nobody was bossy to us and our mother was leading the company on her own with only a couple of employees, so she was the whole time in the factory and Wolf was our leader and we were very naughty."

But there was nobody to chastise Wolfie, nobody to offer praise, either. It is revealing that of all the awards Wolf has received in and out of the wine industry, including the Cross of the Order of Merit from the Federal Republic of Germany in 2006 and the Order of Australia in 2001, he nominates one from a university as the one that means most to him.

In 1996, Charles Sturt University, which educates 80 per cent of Australia's oenologists, awarded him an honorary Doctorate of Applied Science in recognition of his contribution to the wine industry. He was the first Australian winemaker and winery proprietor to receive the honour. "The Order of Australia set me a little bit back emotionally because it never crossed my mind. But I think I was more floored when I got the doctorate from the university. Simply

The Wolf Blass Visitor Centre at Nuriootpa.

Important people in Wolf's life (from left): Jenny Hurley, Bob May, Margaret May, Fred Vella, Yvonne Vella, Dr Michael Hawkes and Merridy Hawkes.

because my father was a double doctor, he had six brothers who also were university graduates in different faculties, and none of us three boys had the qualifications for moving up into this academic grading. So he would have been terribly disappointed in us. And I thought about it when it came my way and this was definitely something which probably got me back to whatever I may have missed – even though it has come later in my life."

Wolf's father was a misfit in the commercially successful family of Otto Sohn, with no business experience at all, but with doctorates in law and economics. On the rare occasions when he was home during Wolf's childhood, he was also a very strict disciplinarian. "I never really understood why my mother, who was such a happy, strong woman, ever fell in love with my father; he was just the absolute opposite. She was a little bit of a

heavy practical person, business orientated and happy and hardworking. And he was very strict. You could never go home and complain that your schoolteacher gave you a whack because then you would get a whack from him, too. I got a hiding every time when the half yearly results came out. They were never any good. I've never failed, but I'll tell you one thing, I was a shocker. I just didn't do homework, despite the fact that they put people behind me, to try to teach me and do all this type of thing." Later, it was different and Friedrich was proud of his son's achievements in Australia. Although, as Raelene noticed, some concerns were expressed about his "living in sin" with her in the Barossa.

Shirley thinks it is Wolf's sense of disappointing his father and mother as a child and young man that make him tick, even down to his need for nurturing. "He loves to be mothered, because of course he didn't really have a mum. She just worked her butt off, I think, and didn't really have a lot of time for the family. So he's constantly making little comments, like, he'll do something for me in the kitchen and he'll come out with, 'Aren't I a good little boy?' And I give him a pat on the back and he's happy as Larry. He just wants to be appreciated."

In the Swiss Alps, at the top before he begins to ski down, he will take time to reflect on old friends now gone. "When you go up the lifts and you sit up there on the mountain, you start going back and you start looking at people I had been affiliated with and they are already gone 10 or 15 years ago and I had to make the eulogy, then I think to myself, 'How lucky am I? I am still here.' You know, this is what goes through your mind, because you're in a different world up there and I am just saying to myself, 'This can't be true.'"

While this biography has provided a chance to look back over his life from the perspective of others as well as his own – and perhaps so he can be even more widely appreciated for his immense achievements in business and the community – Wolf's story seems a long way from a final chapter.

At Wolf Blass Winery, the best of the 2009

Wolf with Chris Hatcher, John Glaetzer and Caroline Dunn, 2004.

vintage has been chosen and the wine is in the making for his 80th birthday celebrations, and there's no way he'd miss that. But even Wolf Blass must bow to the inevitable, at least in terms of the corporeal. "Somebody else has to carry this on, but in the future the Wolf Blass brand is going to be a brand like Coca-Cola. This name, Wolf Blass, will never disappear." WB

Staring down old age

As a healthy man, Wolf really enjoys a mild illness. He has always looked much younger than his years and his energy levels have been extraordinary. He sets himself tough physical challenges, determined to beat the stiffening joints that come with age and prove that he can survive and be fit and strong, even as he sees friends and colleagues decline and die.

One of his favourite sports is skiing in Europe and he does it every year. In early 2009, he took the lifts to more than 4000 metres on one of the great peaks of Switzerland's Zermatt Valley, where the horizon is dominated by the Matterhorn. "It was minus 15 degrees and all down hill and I was with three mates, each of them a ski instructor in his own right and 10-15 years younger." When he reached the top of the mountain and looked over the valley, he felt a great sense of gratitude that he was there at all, when so many friends were dead.

Given his need to push himself so physically hard, it's a measure of how much he loves Shirley that Wolf will go with her on the slowest of holidays on earth – ocean cruises. But the mere act of slowing down often has a dramatic effect. In Edinburgh, on a day trip from a QEII cruise, Wolf complained of pains in his left shoulder. Friends made the mistake of asking whether they extended to his chest, and Wolf quickly decided he must be having a heart attack. An ambulance was called and Wolf was being wired up to all the monitors, but struggling and calling out to Shirley, "Have you got the camera, where is it? You have to take photos." If he is not to be forgotten, not a moment of his life must go unchronicled, even this one.

He was not having a heart attack but a panic attack, compounded by the fact that he had been carrying a backpack that was too heavy on his shoulder. Worse was to come. Wolf, so proud of his health and fitness, was refused permission to return to the ship. "He was devastated by that because they decided he was a health risk," Shirley says. He got no sympathy from her, though. "This is no good, Wolf, you mustn't do this. You are crying, Wolf," she told him.

On another cruise, having absolutely refused to use the hand disinfectants the staff insist for passengers these days, Wolf declared, "Rubbish, I never get sick!"

Suddenly you realise that you cannot bloody run as fast as you thought.

WOLF BLASS

He was struck down by the scourge of cruise ships, norovirus, which causes diarrhoea, stomach pains and vomiting. He was confined to his cabin for four days. "It was the most relaxing trip he ever had," Shirley says.

At the time, Wolf was preparing for interviews for this book and had travelled with material he wanted to review before the project got underway. "He was very happy. He was in his dressing gown, he was lying back on our private deck watching DVDs of himself. He's amazing like that, that he really has to get sick to relax."

Shirley was also by his side when Wolf needed a hernia operation. He checked himself into a suite in a private hospital near the best Chinese restaurant in town so he could order in meals. Given the location of the hernia, in the groin, he expressed some concern to Shirley about whether the surgeon's knife

Wolf in his boardroom reviewing pictures of his life for this book, November 2008. He has about 110 photo albums documenting his life.

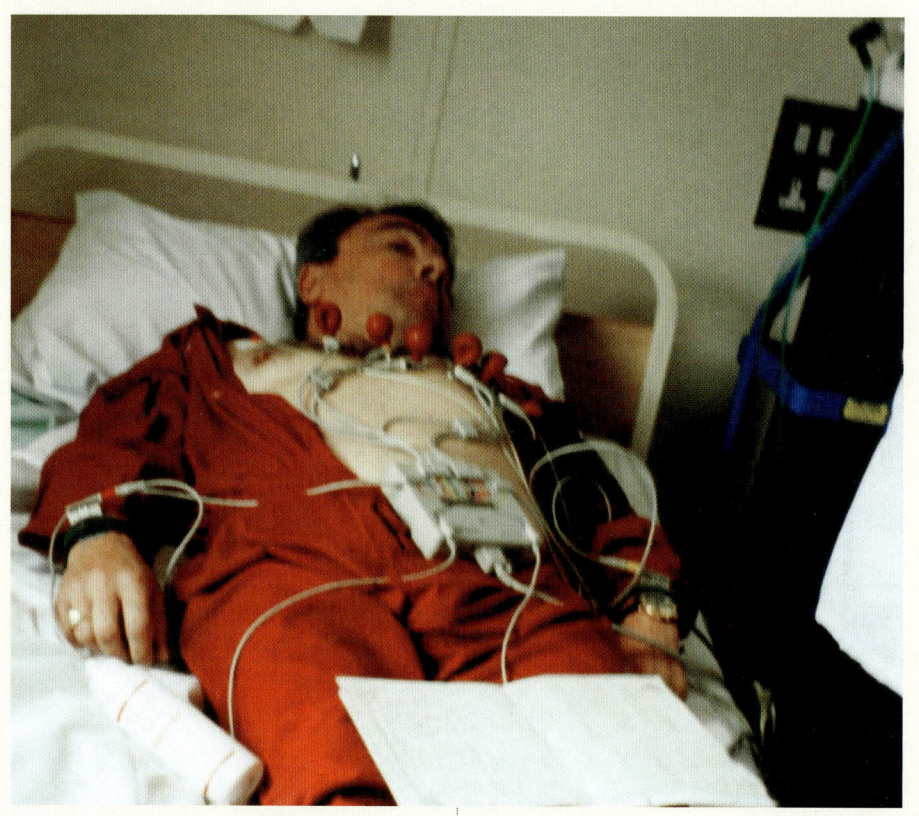

Buchinger Clinic on Lake Constance in southern Germany. Founded in the early 1950s by Dr Otto Buchinger, it offers "therapeutic fasting and integrative medicine" and guarantees "physical and mental regeneration". Wolf's program involves fasting, consuming only a cup of broth, a glass of fruit juice, a spoonful of honey and 100g of fat-free yoghurt a day, as well as drinking 3.5 litres of water and as much herbal tea as he wants. Everyday for a fortnight he takes a 6am walk of six kilometres, then gym work, physio and probably cycling as well.

"I lose about 3.5-4kg, but my mind is 100 per cent. I am switched on like a time-bomb and I am physically fit afterwards to go skiing. Or sometimes I do things in conjunction with promotional activities. I feel that without this I wouldn't probably sit here today. My heart is strong and every three months I have a total blood control check and I look at cholesterol, I look at blood pressure and I have got some tablets for those. I enjoy drinking and I do that, not much during the day, but in the evening, and my liver is still OK – that's an amazing thing with my lifestyle."

Wolf was struck down with norovirus while onboard the QE II with Shirley. "I have worked out that actually he loves a reason to rest and go to bed," she says.

might slip. "Don't worry, I'll leave them a note," Shirley told him. It read: "Don't slip with the knife, look after the little Peter." On the trolley on the way into the theatre, Wolf presented the surgical team with the note and a bottle of Scotch. "When he came back out of the theatre, the doctors had written their note in return, saying that they managed to save it, because they couldn't find it," laughs Shirley.

Every winter for the past 25 years, Wolf has spent two weeks at the

> *Wolf really has to get sick to relax.*
>
> SHIRLEY NYBERG-BLASS

But the clinic is one place Shirley insists on leaving Wolf alone, one of the few things they don't do always together. He takes his brother Fritz instead to keep him company.

"I have been twice with him, but am not overweight and actually I leave the clinic and I need to build myself up," Shirley says. "I prefer not to go on a fasting diet, but I can go there and do like 600 calories or something like that. And I may do that next time with him. It's not my favourite place to spend time, but I will do it with him, because he swears by it and he certainly is doing alright on it."

Wolf has come to enjoy the familiar surroundings after all these years, something Shirley says is important to him. "They all know him and if they change staff he is devastated, he is not happy at all. But he likes to be able to speak the lingo and of course this is why he doesn't particularly want to go to Italy or Greece with me, because he can't speak the language and that is not what he wants."

Despite being so proud of his fitness, Shirley swears Wolf enjoys a mild illness. "If he gets a common cold, he is shocking. He will get into the bedroom – he will go and put his dressing gown on, on top of his clothes, he will get a big, thick towel and wrap it around his neck, he will stuff tissues up each nostril and he will walk around the house the saddest, sorriest little boy in the world and everybody knows that he has got a cold. Anybody that phones, even if they phone for me, he tells them, 'Oh! I am sick.' He is an absolute sook when it comes to having a cold.

"But I have worked out that actually he loves a reason to rest and go to bed and that gives him one. He's got to have an excuse to do that, though, and when he does do that he is in seventh heaven and he rings the bell and he has another cup of tea – you know, he really uses it – he gets the most out of me that he can."

It's an interesting contrast to Wolf the athlete, the man who has to go harder and faster than anyone else around him. In 2004, at the age of 70, he decided to try to win a German Sports Medal for his age group from the German Sports Academy. He had just come from the Buchinger Clinic, followed by a skiing holiday, when he decided to test himself a little harder once he got home to Australia. To win the medal, he had to complete a 200m swim, a 50m sprint, a 10km power walk, a shot-put and standing jumps. "I started training and I just kept training. I would walk in the office every morning, bloody flat-footed. And the funny part of it is, the hard thing was, that swimming isn't one of my best things.

The three amigos
at the Matterhorn:
Leo Hirzel, Wolf and
Bernhard Ryf.

Wolf with Leo and
Lea Hirzel.

"So, anyway, Shirley would be sitting and reading the paper near the swimming pool and I would just be going bloody backwards and forwards [he had to take stroke correction lessons first]. I just absolutely did it my way and when we did this 10km walk, this guy testing me said, 'You are going to be close to a record.' He said, 'Why don't you just take it easy?' He was running out of puff, this bloody bloke. And I equalled the record, so it was good, good fun. And then someone said, 'Are you going to do it again?' No I'm not."

There is, however, one whole-of-life health tip that Wolf gives to anyone who will listen: "If you don't enjoy wine or good food or sex, and you believe you will live longer, you are wrong. Boredom makes you believe that you live longer." He also likes to quote another old saying: "Wine, the cleverest thing God invented after sex. Wine lasts longer and causes infinitely less trouble."

Retirement was not an option as Wolf planned for beyond his 75th birthday in 2009, a tumultuous year and not a particularly good one personally. "This year is in turmoil," he says. "There are some events outside my jurisdiction, which I have to handle, there are also family affairs and I have got businesses to attend to which are run by my children, which they need me more probably than anything else.

"And then this huge promotional activity which is expected of me this year globally and domestically is taking a big slice of my time. Let's hope that by Christmas this year the good, the bad and the indifferent is behind me and I will be looking hopefully at a different phase – from then onwards."

He would like to spend more time in Europe in winter, skiing and enjoying the comfortable familiarity of his first language and the countryside of his childhood and youth. "How can I handle this with my staff is a big question mark, they are relying on a certain income. I am not Mr X who can walk away, this is the unfortunate part. There are a lot of people relying on me."

The unpredictability of the ageing process is a challenge for someone like Wolf, who needs to maintain control over everything. "I should

have done things differently earlier. But how do you know? In the process of ageing, suddenly you realise that you cannot bloody run as fast as you thought.

"Your mind is probably faster, but how do you switch the mode from 3rd gear to 2nd – it's not easy if you are in a healthy mind. If your health fades, then that will determine your destiny, but even if you're 100 per cent healthy and you think, 'Shit, you are doing alright', other people may think, 'He's just an old man, he doesn't know what he's talking about.'"

In modern times, Wolf has added a dislike for email to his lifelong distrust of lawyers and legal contracts. "There is a huge amount of time wasted on the electronics instead of what is most important – the handshake and looking somebody in the eye and making a deal. They do not know how to communicate with people and I think that is where the biggest downturn and downfall in business is today. The lack of personal communication with people.

"I got my first email and I said, 'You've got the telephone. What do you want to bloody talk about?' You

Wolf after winning the German Sports Medal at the age of 70 in 2004.

shake hands with somebody, with your biggest enemy, and if you want to bloody solve a problem you go there, you don't forget their face."

Left: Wolf with friend and Mt Buller snow resort proprietor, Hans Grimus, playing Austrian music.

Wolf with Franz Shellhorn.

Above: Wolf with former South Australian Premier Don Dunstan.

Wolf with Australia's Liberal Opposition Leader, Malcolm Turnbull, 2008.

THE WOLF BLASS JOURNEY

BLASS, Wolfgang Franz Otto

1934 ▶ Born in the village of Stadtilm in the Thuringia Mountains, East Germany

Father Dr Friedrich Blass
Mother Irmgard Sohn
Brothers Fritz (born 1939) and Peter (1944)
Family ties (from mother's side) with the wine and spirit company called Otto Sohn, O.H.G. in Stadtilm and Franz Schellhorn Wine & Apple Juice Co in Arnstadt, situated in Thuringia, the Green Heart of East Germany

1945 - 48 ▶ Attended various high schools in West Germany (due to postwar social and economic problems), although his family was still located in East Germany.

1949 ▶ Completed high school at Heimschule Boarding School, Burg-Neuhaus

1949 – 52 ▶ Apprenticeship in Winemaking & Viticulture with:
- Edmund Diehl, Gau-Odernheim, Rheinhessia
- Heinrich Dubuis, Waldbockelheim, River Nahe

1952 ▶ Certificate in Viticulture & Winemaking issued by Chamber of Agriculture, Bad-Kreuznach, River Nahe

1952 – 53 ▶ Engaged as a qualified expert and gained additional experience in spirit and liquor manufacturing with Hans Schneider & Co in Frankfurt am Main

1954 ▶ Diploma & Oenologist, Wurzburg Wine University
▶ Returned to Hans Schneider & Co for a further year

1955 ▶ Engaged for one year as Wine Expert with Blumenthal Wine & Sparkling Wine Cellars at Large, Linz on River Rhine

1956 ▶ Kellermeister for Karl Finkenauer, Bad Kreuznach, Germany

1957 ▶ Kellermeister Diploma, Chamber of Industry & Trade, Wurzburg Wine University
▶ Wine Chemist for Copenhagen Wine Importers, London

1958 – 60 ▶ Cellar Superintendent for Avery & Co, Bristol, UK

1960 ▶ Job offers as sparkling wine expert in the Barossa Valley, South Australia, or Venezuela, South America

1961 ▶ British Diploma – Wine & Spirits (British Bottler Institute)
▶ Migrated to Australia

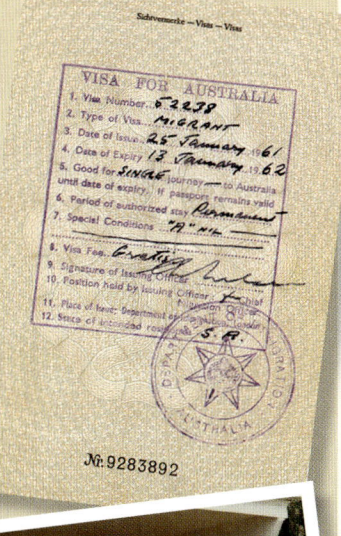

1961 – 63	▶	Sparkling Wines Manager for Kaiser Stuhl Co-operative, responsible for Pearl wines and sparkling wine development
1964 – 69	▶	First freelance Technical Adviser (paid $2.50 an hour). Travelling in his beloved VW, consulted to companies like Woodley's, Norman's, Bleasdale, Clare Valley Co-operative, Jim Barry and Rovalley Wines. Introduced quality table wines into their portfolio and achieved their first gold medals and trophies at national wine shows, including a Jimmy Watson Trophy for Basedow
1966	▶	Registered the business name "Bilyara" (meaning Eaglehawk).
	▶	Produced first vintage of 250 dozen.
	▶	Member of American Society of Oenologists
	▶	Fellow of Marketing Association of Australia and New Zealand
1969 – 73	▶	Manager and Winemaker for United Distillers. Converted Tolleys image from a brandy-producing company into a wine icon by creating the famous Tollana range. Revolutionised the fermentation process in red wine and within three years Tollana (T.S.T.) became one of the most successful red-wine exhibitors in Australia
	▶	Heralded as the Golden Boy in the new era of Australian wine production
	▶	Changed red wine styles through selected oak maturation and made "drinkability" the key word
1973	▶	Resigned after confrontation with United Distillers (T.S.T.) management over his small private production, which was viewed as a conflict of interest

THE BRAND

1973	▶	Started own business – Wolf Blass Wines International – with a $2000 overdraft and a land holding of 1.6 hectares and an old tin shed
1974 – 76	▶	Won three consecutive Jimmy Watsons (Melbourne Wine Show) 1974, 1975, 1976
	▶	Created a sensation and media frenzy when he stated, "My wines make weak men strong and strong women weak!"
	▶	John Glaetzer joins Blass
	▶	Bilyara Vineyards adopts Eaglehawk label
	▶	National distribution network created
	▶	First exports to New Zealand, Fiji, Hong Kong, Singapore, Malaysia and Papua New Guinea

1977 ▶ Developed a new Rhine riesling style (with the addition of grape juice), which became Australia's most preferred Rhine riesling, selling close to two million bottles (AC Nielsen)

1982 ▶ Inducted as a "Baron of the Barossa" for his outstanding contribution to the district, not only to the wine and grape-growing industries, but also the local community over a considerable period

1984 ▶ Wolf Blass Wines goes to a public company with market capitalisation of $15.2 million, Wolf Blass retaining 60 per cent

▶ Receives the IWSC Trophy for the Best Australian Red Wine, presented by IWSC President, Madame Odette Pol-Roger, at the House of Commons, London

1984 – 85 ▶ 3.5 million bottles of Wolf Blass wines sold

1985 ▶ Wolf Blass headquarters opens at 64 Hindmarsh Square, Adelaide

▶ National marketing award for excellence awarded by The Australian Marketing Institute

▶ Marketing and packaging were revolutionised. Bow tie and label description are colour coded

▶ International partnership with Remy Martin, France, and formation of Remy/Blass sales distribution, a national company

1986 ▶ 50 per cent acquisition of the independent Australian Bottling Company, including production of sparkling wine and Champagne styles

1987 ▶ Great South Australian Award for Achievements in Commerce

▶ Awarded the inaugural Qantas Cup (USA v Australia) for the Best Cabernet Sauvignon in the Red Wine Classification

1989 ▶ Finalist in National Business Entrepreneur of the Year Award, Sydney, Australia

1990 ▶ Joint venture with a New Zealand wine company in the Marlborough region, Corbans Wines and Wolf Blass International

▶ By the end of 1990, the number of national and international awards, since the 1966 vintage, totalled 2575, comprising:
  - 135 trophies
  - 712 gold medals
  - 812 silver medals
  - 869 bronze medals
  - 47 diplomas

- ▶ Australia's most successful red-wine exhibitor at National Wine Shows – Sydney, Perth, Melbourne, Adelaide, Brisbane, Hobart and Canberra. Top honour for the ninth time in ten years
- ▶ Joint venture with one of the world's largest wine and spirit manufacturers and distributors, Joseph E. Seagram's & Sons Inc, to create Australia's largest independently owned wine packaging operation with the Wolf Blass Wines International owned Australian Bottling Company
- ▶ Export activities and markets created in 30 different countries, including deals with seven international airlines and various shipping lines

1991
- ▶ Personally initiated Australia's very first public museum of the wine industry – the Barossa Valley Wine Heritage Museum at Bilyara Vineyards

1991
- ▶ Formation of Mildara Blass Limited with market capitalisation of $125 million
- ▶ Appointed as Deputy Chairman Mildara Blass
- ▶ Formation of Wolf Blass Group of Companies implementing various business investments and developments
- ▶ Release of the biography *Wolf Blass – A Journey in Wine*

1992
- ▶ Acclaimed by an independent panel of peers from the global wine industry as International Winemaker of the Year at the International Wine & Spirit Competition in London and awarded the Robert Mondavi Trophy. Wolf Blass was the only Australian winery nominated in the final line-up of 10 international wine producers from countries including France, Italy, Germany, the US, New Zealand and South Africa
- ▶ On the international scene, Wolf Blass as an ambassador has a huge impact on the image and quality of the Australian wine industry

1996
- ▶ Awarded an Honorary Doctorate of Applied Science in recognition of his contribution to wine export development through the 1970s and 1980s, and for his innovative marketing skills that revolutionised wine marketing and packaging within Australia – the first Australian Winemaker and Winery Proprietor ever to receive this honour. The award was bestowed by the Charles Sturt University, which educates 80 per cent of Australian oenologists

| 1997 | ▶ Awarded the inaugural "Legend of Langhorne Creek Honour" by the Langhorne Creek Winemakers and Langhorne Creek Grapegrowers Associations for his outstanding contribution to these industries |

1997 ▶ Awarded the inaugural "Legend of Langhorne Creek Honour" by the Langhorne Creek Winemakers and Langhorne Creek Grapegrowers Associations for his outstanding contribution to these industries

2000 ▶ Awarded the McWilliam's Wines Maurice O'Shea Award, one of the most prestigious awards in the Australian wine industry, for his enormous contribution during his 35-year career. This was the 10th award to be given and, for the first time, not only did a panel of influential industry leaders vote, but so did the previous nine award winners.

2001 ▶ Queen's Birthday honour
▶ Appointed as a Member in the Order of Australia for "service to the development of the Australian wine industry, particularly as an export industry, and to the promotion of excellence in winemaking, viticulture, marketing and research"

2004 ▶ Appointed Vice-President of the prestigious International Wine & Spirit Competition (IWSC), London

2005 ▶ Appointed President 2005 of the International Wine & Spirit Competition and as a consequence received Life Vice President Membership

2006 ▶ The President of the Federal Republic of Germany, Horst Koehler, through the German Ambassador Martin Lutz, presented one of the Government's most prestigious honours and the nation's highest awards – The Cross of the Order of Merit "Das Bundesverdienstkreuz" – for his outstanding contribution to cultural life and nurturing positive relationships/partnerships, over and above, between the German and Australian peoples, cultures and countries
▶ Honoured by the Australian Institute of Export with a Hero Award in recognition of the 2.8 million cases of Wolf Blass brand exported in the previous 12 months

THE CORPORATION

1996 ▶ Foster's acquires Mildara Blass for $560 million (net assets) to add a premium wine division to their globally successful beer empire, however control of the wine sector was fully retained by Mildara Blass management

1999 ▶ The Jimmy Watson Trophy awarded for the fourth time – an historic achievement

2000	▶	Name changed to Beringer Blass Wine Estates, reflecting the $2.6 billion purchase of California-based Beringer Wine Estates, combined with the Wolf Blass multi-million case brand, in order to create a uniform global identity combined with high grade quality vineyards: 7 in the US, 14 in Australia, 2 in New Zealand and 1 in Italy
2001	▶	Completion of the $30 million extension of production facilities at the Wolf Blass Winery, becoming the most advanced premium designed plant, crushing 80,000 tonnes of grapes. The facility was officially opened by then Premier of South Australia, John Olsen
2000 – 2001	▶	Awarded Best Australian Wine Producer by IWSC, London, two years in a row
2002	▶	Awarded the prestigious International Winemaker of the Year by IWSC, London, winning the Robert Mondavi Trophy for the second time, a remarkable achievement competing against more than 4000 entries
2003	▶	Wolf Blass becomes Australia's number one brand by volume and by value
2004	▶	The $5.5 million Wolf Blass Visitor (Tasting) Centre opens in the Barossa Valley
2005	▶	Total Wolf Blass branded products reaches 50 million bottles – 70 per cent for export. Leading brand in Canada, Ireland, UK, Singapore and Hong Kong
	▶	The ultimate award from the International Wine & Spirit Competition, London, recognising the International Winemaker of the Year (formerly known as the Robert Mondavi Trophy) is renamed the Wolf Blass Trophy
	▶	Foster's acquires Southcorp, Australia's largest wine corporation, for $3.2 billion making it the leading premium wine company in the world. Listed on the Australian Stock Exchange. Globally, the new entity trades as: Foster's – Australia, Asia, Pacific Foster's – Americas Foster's – Europe, Middle East, Africa
	▶	The Group sells 500 million bottles and accounts for about a third of Australia's exports and a third of the domestic bottled wine market
	▶	Major markets in the US, Australia, UK, Canada, Ireland, Asia and Scandinavia
2006	▶	Completion of the $75 million bottling and packaging facility at the Wolf Blass Winery in the Barossa Valley with a capacity of 24,000 bottles an hour
	▶	16,000 containers of wine are shipped annually from Port Adelaide, South Australia, for export destinations globally

2007

▶ Wolf Blass Wines the first Australian wine company to introduce the screw-top seal globally. Research by the Wine University of Wurzburg, Germany, on bottled wines over two years has shown no detrimental reduction in CO_2 levels and free SO_2 was reduced by only 10-15ml per litre, a perfect antioxidation process

▶ Major promotional drive and consumer education program throughout Asia, including Singapore, Hong Kong, Korea, Taiwan and Japan (Business Times CEO Club, a 30-minute feature on CNBC and featured on Australian ABC TV program "Talking Heads")

2008

▶ Awarded International Red Winemaker of the Year at the International Wine Challenge (IWC) London, involving a blind tasting of 9000 wines from 40 different countries. The IWC is the world's largest wine competition and this award is a testament to the passion, vision and experience of the entire Wolf Blass winemaking team

2009

▶ Total Wolf Blass branded products approaching 65 million bottles – 76 per cent exported to 60 countries, plus shipping lines and airlines

▶ Leading brand in Canada, Hong Kong, Singapore and Ireland

▶ Australia's No.1 bottled still wine brand by value (AC Nielsen)

▶ In celebration of his 75th birthday, the release of a biography on Wolf Blass commemorating 60 years of winemaking, *Wolf Blass, Behind the Bow Tie: The Man, The Brand, The Foundation*

Wolf's current roles

▶ Executive Chairman of the Wolf Blass Group of Companies

▶ Statesman for Wolf Blass Wines International

▶ Ambassador for the Australian Wine Industry abroad

▶ Chairman of the Wolf Blass Foundation

▶ Life Vice-President of the International Wine & Spirit Competition (London)

▶ Ambassador for the International Riesling Challenge, Canberra

▶ Guest Speaker at numerous national and international events

▶ Director of several diverse business ventures

For further information about Global Affairs, please contact Foster's Corporate Office on +61 (3) 9633 2000

THE FOUNDATION

1994
▶ On his 60th birthday, Wolf established the $1 million Wolf Blass Foundation to assist the wine industry to achieve excellence in winemaking, viticulture and marketing The foundation's four key project areas are:
- Viticultural and oenological research and development
- Wine education
- Wine and health
- Global wine industry profile

1996
▶ Staged the inaugural International Wine & Health Conference ("Medically, is wine just another alcoholic beverage?") in Sydney, attracting prominent national and international epidemiologists and research scientists. Discussion papers and proceedings were published by the foundation and distributed nationally and internationally

1998
▶ Implemented the inaugural annual wine lecturer exchange between Charles Sturt University in Wagga Wagga, Australia, and the Wurzburg Wine University in Germany

▶ Sponsored the inaugural Taste Theatres at Wine Australia 1998 in conjunction with the Australian Society of Wine Education. This biennial sponsorship continued in 2000, 2002, 2004 and 2006

2000
▶ Inaugural and on-going sponsor of the International Riesling Challenge in Canberra to revitalise and promote the image of riesling. Introduction of the annual Wolf Blass Award recognising major contributions to the development and promotion of riesling in Australia

▶ Joint venture between the Wolf Blass Foundation and the National Wine Centre to interview and record the memories of Australia's wine industry pioneers and characters who have played significant roles in its development. Conducted by renowned historical consultant Rob Linn, 180 interview tapes and transcripts have now been lodged with the State Library of South Australia and form a valuable resource. This project is of significant importance to the Australian wine industry, is a one-off in the world and cannot be matched for size, quality or diversity of information

2005
▶ Conducted an educational tasting of 51 selected rieslings from all regions of Germany, for a panel of legendary Australian riesling makers. The official Australian wine magazine, *Winestate*, publishes a 12-page feature distributed to 180 publication houses globally

| 2007 | ▶ | Renowned wine writer Max Allen is commissioned to write an historical book on the Australian wine industry based on the oral interviews with wine industry pioneers. Due for release in 2009 |
| 2009 | ▶ | Future vision of the Trustees of the Wolf Blass Foundation – to create a legacy to honour and recognise the icons of the wine industry |

PAST & PRESENT AFFILIATIONS

Wine industry:

- Chairman and judge at international and national wine competitions
- Founder, Past Chairman and Past Managing Director of Wolf Blass Wines International
- Past Board Member of the Barossa Valley Winemakers and Australian Wine & Brandy Producers Association
- Past Promotions Director – Barossa Valley Vintage Festival
- Past Deputy Chairman, Mildara Blass Limited
- Baron of the Barossa
- Life Member Barossa Valley Bacchus Club
- Commandeur Noosa Bacchus Club

CLUBS, INSTITUTIONS & ASSOCIATIONS

- Life Member Junior Chamber of Commerce
- Past Board Member of South Australian Tourist Commission
- Number One Ticket Holder of Norwood Football Club & Past Chairman of the President's Group
- Ambassador and Past Vice-President Adelaide Football Club
- Member of South Australian Racehorse Owners' Association
- Active Sponsor and Member of Balaklava, Gawler & Barossa Valley, Darwin, South Australian and Kangaroo Island Racing Clubs
- Patron and Inaugural Life Member Kangaroo Island Racing Club
- Patron Gawler & Barossa Jockey Club
- Past President, Life Member & International Ambassador of Carbine Club of South Australia
- Senator and Life Member of South Australian German Club
- Founder and Member of Corporate Members German Association
- Life Member Karnevals Group – German Club
- Life Member Italian Club
- Past President and current Member of Barossa Valley Greenock Business Luncheon Club
- President and current Member of Rascal Social Club
- Current Member of Fun Yow Social Club
- Active Member of Victorian Ski Club
- Active Member of Adelaide Pistol & Shooting Club
- Current Member of Adelaide Sailing Club
- Past Secretary Barossa Valley Car Club

WOLF'S FIVE PRINCIPLES FOR SUCCESS

If you are not hands-on, you will be failing.

If you have got a rotten apple amongst the trees – clear it out sooner rather than later.

Don't borrow money if you know you can't pay it back.

Don't believe for a moment that you can make a fast buck in the shortest possible time.

In a partnership, if you haven't got control of 51 per cent (even in your private life) it will fail eventually and it is going to bite physically, mentally, in whichever capacity you are operating in.